SOCIETY-C

To everyone brave enough.

CONTENTS

References available from 136 to 170

They paved paradise and put up a parking lot.

Joni Mitchell

INTRODUCTION

Reality's hard.

And yet, despite living in the most technologically advanced age in history, this technology has, instead of empowering us, placated us.

We're told we have the tools to do whatever we want; that we possess the ability to succeed; that our access to information and resources means that to fail is a sign of something worse: *failure against all odds*; odds which, we're told, are now stacked in our favour by virtue of a mobile phone and a broadband connection.

In the past, we could plead ignorance or bad luck. Today, excuses have vanished in the night; vanquished by the white knight of Google.

Failure is impossible. Success is guaranteed. If we fail, it's our fault: we have the resources. No excuses.

This is the world we're up against; the narrative imposed by global tech and a society that's bought into a myth that technology is – somehow – both our ticket out of reality *and* our ability to change it. This duplicity of technology – as both an agent of change and a way of escape – is the nature of society-on-demand.

How did we get here?

Society-on-demand is our escape; a retreat from the physical world and the demands of physical society; a recognition that over the past thirty years, substantial political and technological change have transformed the way society operates, affecting not just how we spend our time but how we relate to our selves and each other.

Millennials have, until now, experienced the worst of this: growing up in the ashes of the labour movement, the "War on Terror," the 2008 financial crash, the rise of personal devices, through Brexit and – today – through the pandemic; consolidating the previous issues of the last thirty years into a kind of horrible, societal, Collateralised Debt Obligation; an amalgamation of crises for future generations.

And yet, for Gen Z, it's even worse; trading the crumbs of the noughties for the giblets of the 2010s.

Gen Z grew up in a world where fast internet was expected; where smartphones were a normal part of adolescence and where society-on-demand was, itself, society. The waning importance of in person relationships and real-life events – not least a tolerance of those we might disagree with – is a direct consequence of our ability to say and hear what we like in the ethereal realm of the Online, a sanitised space for unchallenged opinion and undisputed thoughts.

Gen Alpha, if you hadn't guessed, is even worse. Growing up in the wake of the pandemic and now facing major difficulties in their development, the damage of lockdowns to children under five is serious. In a study of 58 schools, almost all children who began school in Autumn 2020 struggled with "communication and language development", "personal, social and emotional development" and literacy, with 76% claiming to need "more support than children in previous cohorts."[1]

For Gen Alpha, the pandemic has meant severely limited (if not completely denied) physical contact; and this will remain the case if society-on-demand continues to encroach on physical space. When three in four 18 to 34 year olds prefer digital communication to communication in person, with almost 70% preferring text to phone calls, it's clear that without a dramatic reset, this will only get worse.[2]

Given the crises we've faced and the lack of solutions to the problems they've caused, are we really surprised by our desire to escape? That we prefer the perceived comfort of Instagram and TikTok to the physical reality of our lives? That porn, TV, movies and sports are ever-present, as we cling on with both hands?

These crises have established a rejection of reality. A reality in which our problems are unsolved; where hope, meaning and fulfilment are replaced by apathy, irrelevance and despair; where the malaise of the present is experienced on a daily basis and where – instead of anticipating a resplendent future – we are, instead, resigned to it.

If the future holds nothing for us and the present is so lacking, then we seek comfort in the only place left: the past. We have a nostalgia for moments we've never experienced; histories we've never lived.

In 2021, almost twice as many adults preferred the past to the future. Indeed, the only demographic to prefer the future was 18 to 24 year olds (by a mere 3%), and this appears to be a pandemic induced phenomenon, having preferred to live in the past by 14% in 2019[3] – and it's not surprising.

The Resolution Foundation's *Double Trouble* report showed "a number of structural changes over the past 20 years made young people especially vulnerable to the current crisis" and that "young people have been hard hit compared to other age groups during the pandemic when it comes to both economic security and mental health."[4]

Growing up in the wake of the financial crash followed by ten years of austerity, trebling tuition fees and the degradation of services, coupled with poor wages and job insecurity leading to a mental health crisis (more than half of 18 to 24 year olds had mental health problems in April 2020, versus less than one in three 2018-19); it would be a miracle if these changes did anything but hammer them into the ground.[5]

Combine this with a definitive switch from physical society to society-on-demand through the ubiquity of personal devices, digital entertainment and a distinct lack of hope; it's easy to conclude Gen Z is the most oppressed generation the West has ever seen. Consequently, without radical and immediate change, this oppression will become worse, leaving future generations in a technological, economic and societal death spin.

With a future this brittle and the security of the past allowing only brief respite from the afflictions of the present, we're presented with a choice: entertainment or reality in all its struggle.

We have to deal with the reality at hand: but this is impossible under the current circumstances. The interests of Digital Entertainment are too entrenched. These interests are not the audience it seeks to entertain. On the contrary, to put the interests of the audience above "content" would result in a less profitable industry, hampering growth and boosting the intelligence and awareness to resist it.

The industry relies on the fantasies of its audience. It relies on our ignorance and, fundamentally, it depends on our lack of meaning. We have no alternative – no answer – to the trash we consume. There's a void in our lives: and we don't know how to fill it. Instead, we're easily hijacked; commandeered by flashing images, violence and explicit content: and we can't stop watching.

In 2020, UK adults spent five hours and forty minutes a day watching video content, with an hour and five minutes of this dedicated to streaming services like Amazon Prime. In 2020, more than half of all households were subscribed to Netflix.[6]

These are all increases on 2019 and, although the pandemic has clearly played a part in boosting consumption, many of these trends are expected to continue (55% of adults said they expected to spend as much time watching streamed content as they did during lockdown, and the vast majority expected to continue their subscriptions to Netflix, Amazon Prime and Disney+).[7]

But is it all bad news?

As you might have guessed, increased consumption has fuelled economic growth.

In 2018, the digital sector was responsible for nearly 8% of the UK economy, with year-on-year growth of 7.9% – five times larger than the economy as a whole.[8]

But there were consequences.

In the same year, UK adults were physically active for just 1 hour 30 minutes a week, spending 8 times longer watching on-demand TV and 11 times longer glued to their phones and tablets: and it's expected to get worse.[9]

Consumer spending on streaming is expected to rise 8% a year between 2021 and 2025 – a rise of almost 40% on 2020[10] – in a society where 88% of 5 to 7 year olds use their devices to watch video-on-demand and 99% of 12 to 15 year olds use video sharing platforms.[11]

When the majority of kids use their phones to go online, access to the increasing dominance of digital entertainment is not only going to increase, accelerating consumption: it's also going to expose more children (and adults) to damaging forms of media like pornography, self-harm and other forms of violence. Already, more than one in four 8 to 11 year olds have been exposed to "worrying or nasty content online", as well as almost one in three 12 to 15 year olds).[12]

Digital entertainment providers – whether they're streaming platforms, video-on-demand services or social media – are seen as a liberating force and a beacon of choice: yet they're increasingly accessible to children, embedding greater consumption across all age groups and establishing long term use in Gen Z and Gen Alpha, securing future profits at their expense.

In the absence of parents limiting the devices available to their children (more than half of 5 to 15 year olds own their own smartphone, despite parents' concerns over internet use),[13] we come to a curious impasse: parents provide their kids with the tools to access the internet, yet only a third of them use controls to limit their access to harmful content. Of course, even if they did, the vast majority of children could take their devices outside the home and access the internet elsewhere, even if the home was properly regulated.

In an increasingly "connected" world, where expectations of consumption and online presence continue to pressure young people (one in five girls aged 15 to 18 felt under more pressure to be online *all the time* during 2020's lockdown),[14] the only way to curb the use of these services is to fundamentally reassess their value.

The inability of parents to control the consumption of their own children and their refusal to regulate household (or even their own) use, tells us the first line of defence – the family and the home – has failed, and that curbing the use of these devices is increasingly unlikely. According to the Young Gamers and Gamblers Education Trust, even if parents did seek to control their children's use to reduce harmful content, the crossover between R rated content and video games makes it "almost impossible to monitor a young person's media intake without restricting every form of entertainment", with "reports from primary schools in the UK saying that children have been recreating Squid Game in the playground."[15] Society-on-demand and the damage it inflicts is, seemingly, inescapable.

In times of social crisis, governments need to act. And yet, governments have shown a distinct lack of interest; choosing instead to allow Big Tech a free ride, a battering ram at the foundations of society.

Any criticism of these companies is reserved for specific elements of their practice, not their metastasising and socially destructive nature.

Concerns over data privacy, unfair pricing and taxes have been the main points of discussion; yet the ethos of these companies is rarely questioned. The *Online Safety Bill* is an attempt to address some of the most pernicious effects of online content (preventing anonymous abuse, criminal sanctions on executives and, most importantly, forcing a duty of care on companies to protect users from harmful content).[16] And yet, attempting to regulate the company – not the product or the nature of our devices – shows how disinterested the government really is.

Even if Facebook were to reduce the visibility of harmful content, this would presumably exclude provocative selfies, clenched bums and chiselled biceps; content fuelling the culture behind eating disorders, body dysmorphia and other illnesses.

Would the government really ban attention seeking on Twitter, twerking on TikTok or Faux-Pas on Facebook? Doubtful.

The nature of the digital entertainment industry today is ever-present and compulsive. It's designed for continuous use and, as should be obvious: it's working.

We're spending almost a third of our waking hours on our devices; placated by a seemingly infinite supply of TV shows, movies, music, football and pornography.

So why, given that we're incapable of regulating ourselves, isn't the government doing anything to address it?

Because it's convenient.

The government refuses to curb access because it's quite happy to entrench ignorance, apathy and disengagement. The elevation of digital entertainment is essential to its existence; allowing it to operate with impunity.

When the Prime Minister turns the £2.6m press briefing room into a cinema, it should be clear what his priorities are.[17]

If the industry continues to grow; if content becomes increasingly easy to access through smartphones and personal technology; if children escape the watchful eyes of their parents believing they can forge a career for themselves through the curation of online identities; and if they can get by without ever having to engage in a proper conversation: then the disabilities created and lives ruined by a largely unregulated, instantly accessible digital entertainment industry, will have been worth it.

Facebook, Google, Snapchat, ByteDance and Twitter – not to mention the smartphone enablers of Apple and Samsung, among others – will continue to reap the rewards of an ever-dependent generation; allowing government to benefit at the ballot box, empowered to act in increasingly opaque and tyrannical ways through the plasticity and cynicism of an apathetic public.

In a world of immense digital content, ignorance is not an excuse: and yet, it's increasingly voluntary. It's far easier to retreat into the cave of consumerism, scroll away our concerns from the real world and replace them with new anxieties from the Online.

The snowballing of digital entertainment, its control over our lives, is a gift to those in power; be they private companies or government departments.

We are strangers; isolated and repressed in a society which teeters on the brink of collapse, a generation without hope and low expectations; a society of economic and cultural death. The social contract has ended: and digital entertainment is preventing us from mounting a serious challenge against those responsible, be they systems or people.

Our retreat into society-on-demand has caused us to check out of our lives. We prefer our reality spoon fed: our reality of mythical hope, false meaning and fake identity.

This is about stripping away the weeds of a pervasive digital entertainment industry – the default of an online existence – to rehumanise ourselves and, consequently, achieve the political changes we need.

It is – in short – an argument against society-on-demand; and a call to confront the demands on society.

PROGRESS

*Our inventions are wont to be pretty toys, which distract
our attention from serious things. They are but improved
means to an unimproved end. We are in great haste to
construct a magnetic telegraph from Maine to Texas; but
Maine and Texas, it may be, have nothing important to
communicate.*

Henry David Thoreau.[18]

In Disney World's *Carousel of Progress*, the audience
moves around a central stage. The stage covers four periods
of time, hosting scenes from the early 1900s, the 1920s, late
40s and an unknown point in the future. Each scene follows
a family of animatronics who grow and develop with each
period.

For example, in the early 1900s, the father raves
about new inventions such as movies, the expansion of the
railroads, 20 ft. skyscrapers and "some kind of flying
contraption" which, he assures us, "will never work."

After hailing the virtues of gas lamps and coal-heated
water, he reminds the audience that all of this (including the
water pump in the kitchen sink) is "thanks to progress".

The rest of the scene highlights cultural attitudes of
the time, including flippant misogyny against his daughter
who, upon seeing the audience while getting dressed,
complains she's "indecent."

"Don't worry, Patricia," says the father. "They're
friends!"

Of course, no Disney attraction would be complete
without a song so, at the end of each scene, the family
sings...

*There's a great big, beautiful tomorrow
Shining at the end of every day.
There's a great big, beautiful tomorrow,
And tomorrow's just a dream away.
Man has a dream and that's the start.
He follows his dream with mind and heart,*

And when it becomes a reality,
It's a dream come true for you and me.

So there's a great big, beautiful tomorrow
Shining at the end of every day.
There's a great big, beautiful tomorrow,
Just a dream away.[19]

The audience rotates to the next scene, and repeat. You can imagine the rest.

The 20s pine after jazz, electricity and the efficiency of long-distance train travel.

The 40s extol the virtues of radio, the "rat race" and the refrigerator. And, finally, in "the future", kids are seated around the TV, playing video games, while the father makes Christmas dinner (a punishment for his misogyny in the 1920s, we presume). Of course, being "in the future", the oven now takes voice commands which, once the video game scores are spoken out loud, turns the temperature to 975 degrees, burning the turkey.

As you might have guessed, the *Carousel of Progress* isn't just a list of "achievements." It's a social commentary on outdated attitudes, technology and, above all, what "progress" actually means.

Is it the "rat race" of the long commute? Indeed, when the father complains about driving to and from work, his wife says, "That's what they call progress, dear", to which he reluctantly agrees, before comforting himself with the idea of the TV which, for all its faults, "Gives you something to do after you come home."

The beauty of the *Carousel of Progress* isn't its giddy optimism or charming animatronics: it is, instead, its ability to show progress of value; major developments in the 1900s which brought genuine convenience and benefits to the way we live, such as refrigeration, clean water in the home and, eventually, shared duties and respect between husband and wife; versus progress which, at first, seems harmless and progressive but, on further reflection, seems deeply regressive (automated ovens, meaningless TV, commuting for work and so on).

And yet, the most interesting thing about the *Carousel of Progress* is that, as time goes by, progress becomes mostly regressive. Once basic needs have been addressed, the rest of our "progress" focuses on leisure and entertainment, often to the detriment of both.

Fundamental to this regression is the desire for an easy life; a life unburdened by the inconvenience of boredom; divorced from the simple pleasures of the natural world and human experience: love, service, challenge and creation.

In today's world, it's easy to forget where we came from and how far we've travelled in the past twenty – let alone a hundred – years. The *Carousel of Progress* is an important reminder.

And yet, in the wake of the pandemic, I would argue that what we need isn't so much a carousel of progress, but a carousel of regress. In many ways, the more we've "progressed," the more regressive we've become.

Like the voice-activated oven, we're building "convenience" and "efficiency" into everything for the promise of an easier life.

Our history is one of the continued refusal to assess where we are; to review our "achievements," to analyse whether any of them are, actually, any good. In the words of *Jurassic Park*'s Ian Malcolm: "Scientists were so preoccupied with whether or not they could, that they didn't stop to think if they should."[20]

New Era

As a Millennial, I've lived two lives.

First, a life in the real world – a world of physical existence, presence and human engagement. A world where you'd knock on a friend's door, meet someone on time or face the anxious wait of silence, wondering where they were; a world where the most entertainment your phone could provide was Snake 2 and a prank call.

Like the first, the second exists in the real world; but this is a world of physical separation, absence and hostility. A world which takes place, primarily, online.

Since then, the very existence of an instant, mobile means of communication has allowed us to be late more than ever. Progress which should have reduced our tardiness has, instead, emboldened our lateness. In our decency, we message ahead of time by how late we're going to be, to express how sorry we are; a culture where it's better to be late than show up on time in the first place.

We've transferred the balance of power from conversation to digital messaging. In our delusion, we tell ourselves messages are better because they're "physical" evidence of our care and concern. After all, how would we show our concern if we were on time in the first place?

Our action is sacrificed to prove that we care. "Doing" is no longer important; what matters is claiming to feel a certain way. We view the "content" on our phones as more real than the nuanced, human, relational subtlety of an in person meeting. And that means our sense of community – of healthy, human relationships – has changed.

Like the kid who knocks on a friend's door without an invitation or the parent who ventures across the street for a splash of milk: the previous absence of remote, personal devices necessitated a physical closeness and interaction, requiring a basis of mutual understanding, openness and respect.

The kid who knocks on a friend's door knocks because it's the only way to spend time together. The parent who asks a favour does so knowing their neighbour would do the same. Our reliance on physicality meant building in person relationships was required, not chosen – just as it had been (and still is in many places) for all human existence – allowing spontaneous interaction based on trust.

Today, physical spontaneity's gone; our actions, pre-empted.

Like the text we send to prolong our delay, we build anxiety into our lives; always asking ahead, wondering what someone will think or how it will seem – and yet, we have no problem searching for people online, trawling through their past to justify our rejection.

We're allergic to phone calls and afraid of coffee. In person meets are the preserve of the office. We no longer know how to hold a conversation, maintain eye contact or leave our phones in our pockets.

We've no interest in the "stranger" unless we can manage and limit their interaction with us. We want all the benefits of a relationship with none of its hardship: relationships on our own terms, ensuring others fit into our own idea of personal space, of distance and convenience. The physical world doesn't allow it, so we limit our relationships to the Online; we put our efforts into cultivating a "presence," a "community," a "following."

In the digital world, we control our relationships. We determine who's important. We can mute, block, even switch off our phones (but, let's be honest, most of us would rather die).

It's the reason for self-service check-outs, online shopping, silent discos and dating apps. It's not that they're convenient in themselves: it's that they allow us to avoid the inconvenience of in person reality.

We want the benefits of the world without its problems – and yet its problems are exactly what make us human.

If we have this level of control online, why would we want to take part in a society which offers almost no control at all? A society where the control we have is almost entirely determined by our economic and physical circumstance? Why would we want to be part of that system when we can create and curate an entirely new, parallel society; where our previous identity, circumstance and economic power are, at least in theory, obsolete?

-

In *The Good Place*, after spending thousands of years in Hell, the show's heroes finally make it to Heaven. And yet, upon arrival, they encounter the unexpected: its residents are sick of it.

Heaven is so perfect – so convenient – that everyone wants to leave.

And so, a plan is made to build a way out: an exit door. This door allows people, whenever they're ready, to die. They can walk through it and enter Nothing.

For a while, the very existence of this door – the possibility of ending one's life – is enough motivation to allow most residents to enjoy themselves again. The knowledge that they can choose to die at any time – that there is a way out – gives meaning to their existence. And yet, even this wears off.

One of the main protagonists, Chidi Anagonye, manages to squeeze out a couple of thousand years before, finally, walking through the door.[21] So what was missing?

Struggle, triumph, effort: *Reality*.

The problem was not the existence of heaven, but that it bore such little resemblance to the reality of life on Earth that, no matter how perfect, they no longer wanted to be there; choosing death over an existence which didn't conform to their lived experience.

This is the state of things today.

We have, as a society, lost the ability to accept struggle and inconvenience. Society has promised simplicity, and yet there's a disconnect between our experience online and its execution in person.

Society now requires the distraction of our phones – a continuous, digital leash – in order to operate effectively. Smartphones are becoming fundamental to the way society operates.

Consider something as simple as ordering coffee. We're now actively discouraged from ordering in the cafe itself because orders require staff and queues require space. Solution? Mobile order. And, if you weren't convinced: "Download our app and we'll give you points." And, before we know it, we have apps and loyalty schemes for everything, complementing an already exhaustive list of newsletters, promotional offers and e-mails.

The "convenience" of digital services misaligns with the reality of physical, in person processes. Ordering's easy but the execution is, often, terrible; like a coffee that takes twenty minutes to arrive, restaurants serving cold food or "unexplained items in the bagging area." These things drive us insane because they're breaking the deal we thought we made. We were promised convenience, less stress and cheaper prices; but when we encounter the incompetence of cost cutting and the fallibility of machines over human beings, it all falls apart.

And so, not only does the smartphone user, online shopper or self-checkout user suffer through the mismatch of the ordering process and the receipt of goods and services: but the person who, knowing these problems, wishes to stay away from automated systems and, instead, engage with another human being, is punished through longer wait times, out of stock items and incessant suggestions to "open in app" versus "stay in browser."

This is capitalism: the verge of an aneurism for the reasonable execution of basic things.

Not only do we live in a divided society for resources (assets, wealth and income): we now live in a system based on those engaging with "smart" technology (willing to sacrifice their data, compromise their mental health and weaken their relationships) at the top; benefiting from access to faster, more convenient services (and, with it, cheaper deals): versus those at the bottom who, for whatever reason, do not own or refuse to use technology for these purposes and, therefore, queue to receive slower, inconvenient services, often at a higher price, or are denied service altogether.

Space Without Place

If the real world is now online, then it's no surprise the physical one's falling apart. Climate change is allowed to get worse because we no longer see a link between the planet and our own existence. Our regard for the natural world is a low priority because we no longer believe it has anything to offer. We may, intellectually, recognise a link between the planet's health and our own – that we rely on sustainable ecosystems for healthy lives: yet we've forgotten what a healthy life looks like. We see more value in our personal devices, streaming services, sport and social media than the natural world. We believe the world has nothing of interest to offer us versus the promise of "online content."

We are butterflies in reverse, cocooning ourselves in computers, emerging only able to crawl. We believe the Online matters more than physical space, more than the beauty of the natural world; more than the physical exhilaration of ocean swims and thunderstorms. Today, we see everything through the prism of online values.

These values objectify the real world, transforming it into a vehicle for online content. We live our lives in the promise that we'll share them online and we experience life through the prison of a six-inch screen, reducing everything to "content."

Nothing is real unless it's recorded. Nothing's worth doing if there's no evidence of enjoying it (especially if we can't take our own images).

There's no mystery or development. No room for change. Everything is reviewed, experienced and evidenced (and, if it's not, we *definitely* won't be doing *that*).

What began as a well-meaning place to share information has, like the world offline, been corrupted by the demands of the free market, transforming it into a tool of oppression – a tool we now carry with us – playing a fundamental role in our lives as an accelerator of consumerism offline. We objectify everything and experience nothing.

The "progress" we've achieved has allowed society to migrate to a seemingly non-physical place, a place we value more than the physical society in which we live.

And yet, the internet *is* a physical place, relying on servers, satellites, masts, computers and undersea cables. Just ask the people of Tonga, whose undersea fibre-optic cable was severed during the tsunami of January 2022.[22]

Countries around the world rely on deep-sea cables for connectivity, providing 99% of the world's communication traffic. [23] If one of these cables breaks, internet connectivity becomes very difficult, using satellites instead and resulting in slow, intermittent services. Without a satellite connection, there's no connectivity: the internet does not exist.

But it's not just natural disasters that threaten the infrastructure of the Online. In 2013, three men were arrested in Egypt for intentionally cutting a major undersea cable[24] and, in 2008, 70% of all internet and phone traffic was compromised after a ship's anchor severed a string of cables linking Europe, Africa and Asia, affecting 75 million people.[25]

Of course, certain countries are better-connected than others, with multiple cables connecting Western countries, in particular. (The UK is connected to fifty of them.)[26]

Many of these cables are funded by Big Tech companies like Google, Facebook, Amazon and Microsoft; benefitting from increased traffic and high speeds.[27]

The presumption of connectivity – that it will always be around, that it's immune to physical inconveniences like *the planet* – is a farce.

Besides the ability to disrupt the physical infrastructure of the web, we have to ask who benefits. If Big Tech invests millions into connectivity, then we can be pretty sure they're going to be the main beneficiaries.

Society-on-demand relies on the myth that it's just as stable – just as real – as physical society. If it didn't, we wouldn't be wasting so much of our time there.

Instead, society-on-demand – even if its physical infrastructure remains functional – remains in the control of Big Tech through ads, algorithms and data: and that means society-on-demand doesn't work in our interests, nor can we have an equal relationship with its controllers, nor any say in its decisions. The internet is the realm of private companies, not elected officials (officials who, as we'll see, are only too happy to let them do as they please).

And yet, society-on-demand remains our escape. It remains our focus. It is, as we've seen, omnipresent. As such, it remains our society of choice despite its problems: and it's not surprising.

We live in a society which doesn't work. We know our chances of a meaningful life are almost zero; not because the circumstances might elude us (although, they might), nor because of a foreseen lack of security: but because we have no idea what a meaningful life looks like.

In a world where our basic needs are, for the most part, met and where, in immediate society, most of us can hope to not starve to death: we have too much time to be free.

Meaning eludes us because we have time to think about it. Our lives are unfulfilled with a void in the middle and materialism, success, fame and influence have promised a way of escape.

But a life of struggle is its own concern. We're preoccupied with hardship. Our meaning in life is to live.

Even without the comfort of a more affluent existence – without the security of decent pay, secure housing and good health – we find ourselves desperate to escape; not through the simple joys of relationship, nature and creative endeavour; but through social media, football, pornography, TV, movies, etc.

We've lost sight of the things which make life worth living because most of us have never experienced them.

We need to see the circus of consumerism for what it is: spiritual and physical death, empowered further by society-on-demand; the cause and response to the demands on society: our exit door.

We live in a society where the solution to boredom, depression and anxiety is not to stop producing: it's to produce more things. We're deprived of nothing – except nothing.

We're no longer allowed to content our selves with simple pleasures. To do so would ruin an economy built on excess and regressive technology.

And yet, there's one invention, in particular, which has fundamentally changed our relationship with each other and who we are as individuals: the smartphone.

REVOLUTION

Every once in a while, a revolutionary product comes along and changes everything.

Steve Jobs.[28]

In 2007, Apple launched the iPhone.[29]

The iPhone was, according to Jobs, "a revolutionary and magical product that is literally five years ahead of any other mobile phone."[30]

This was an understatement.

Not only would the iPhone revolutionise the smartphone: it would revolutionise how society functions, how we relate to each other and how we relate to ourselves.

We are all born with the ultimate pointing device— our fingers—and iPhone uses them to create the most revolutionary user interface since the mouse.[31]

With the reduction of human beings to mere users of technology, and our fingers – the result of millions of years of evolution and growth; of dexterity, resourcefulness and expression – demoted to a mere "pointing device", the iPhone became the first of what we now consider extensions of our selves; not just physically, but emotionally.

Advertised as "an iPod, a phone, and an internet communicator",[32] the iPhone focused on a single idea: to streamline all our devices into one product: to make our lives easier.

And who wouldn't want that? Efficient, useful and dynamic: a device to entertain and connect; listen to music, browse the internet and, of course, make and receive phone calls.

And yet, revolutionary as it was, it wasn't until a few years later, with the rise of social media and fast internet speeds, that issues began to emerge...

Availability

The smartphone is not an issue in itself.

To claim that there's nothing good about it, nothing of value; that it's delivered no societal benefit whatsoever, would be dismissive at best.

The presence of a camera in the hands of ordinary people on a device which can both record, photograph, store, edit and upload information in seconds is a safeguard against police brutality and other injustices.

The role of citizen journalism, through sharing information and analysing events, is fundamental to the advancement of radical political change and holding power to account. Smartphones have an important role to play.

The ability to connect with each other, to share information in real time and document events through a camera are important tools in a society where institutions and systems do not always have sufficient photo or video evidence (and, even if they did, could we trust they'd remain free of manipulation or even turned on in the first place?)

These systems are presumptively immune from prosecution; the killing of Breonna Taylor should make that abundantly clear; her death resulting in the local police department being forced to wear body cameras.[33]

George Floyd's *murder*, on the other hand, was a murder because it was recorded. Without video evidence, who's to say if Chauvin would have been found guilty? History suggests he wouldn't, joining a long list of "killings," with no accountability.

Even something as basic as staying in touch with family and friends is, when used correctly, a major benefit of the smartphone and the internet in general (although, it should be noted, this isn't always the case. A recent study on the effects of lockdown and the use of digital media found the more elderly people engaged with others virtually, the more likely they were to be lonely and – significantly – suffered more loneliness than those without any contact at all).[34]

The problem, as we've seen, occurs when the smartphone is used to displace our relationships and physical reality through the dominance of society-on-demand; a platform for regressive amusement through aggressive engagement.

And this is far too easy; the consequence of its ubiquity, as an extension of our selves, has a direct impact on the viability of society, mental health and political change.

Despite possessing the tools to change our lives, these tools are, instead, changing us.

Stealing the Moment

I'm old enough to remember the TV guide.

Growing up, we'd spend hours going through the Christmas edition, scouring each page for the best shows, biros in hand, making plans to fit around our favourite films. Our entertainment was planned days – often weeks – in advance.

Whether it was *Indiana Jones* at 4, *Home Alone* at 3:15, or *The Muppet Christmas Carol* at 7:35; we'd run downstairs, jump on the sofa (or the floor, if you weren't so lucky) and sit around the TV as a family; enjoying not just the films but the reactions of each other: the excitement, the tension, the hilarity of Marv falling down a hole or the bizarre elation of Ebenezer Scrooge dancing with a giant, ginger muppet.

But it's only recently I've come to appreciate just how human – in their radical simplicity – these moments were. Today, our level of choice and personalisation, not just of entertainment but of our devices themselves, has established an environment in which families can be in the same room but oblivious to each other; where everyone feels able to "do their own thing." On the occasions we do things together, we absent-mindedly check our phones every few minutes because we couldn't possibly do just *one thing* for all that time. According to a 2018 survey of 2,000 adults, more than half of us check our phones at least "fairly frequently" while watching TV, rising to an average of 77% for 18 to 34 year olds.[35] This exemplifies a wider attention crisis affecting young people in particular, with 4 out of 5 using subtitles all or part of the time. Originally created for those with hearing difficulties, subtitles have become "an essential aid for following a show for many people; especially if other distractions and devices are competing for their attention."[36]

And this attention deficit, this inbuilt distraction, has become a cultural phenomenon, one which is now deeply ingrained in society. In 2015, the majority of adults said it was unacceptable to check their phone at dinner, but 42% admitted checking it anyway.[37] Just three years later, this had risen by more than a quarter, to 54%.[38]

With a device that's almost as easy to check as not check, as easy to pick up as it is to leave alone; is it any surprise we're addicted?

Apple devised a product which was so easy to use that compulsive use was inevitable.

A device this well designed, this aesthetically pleasing, this functional, was always going to elevate the phone from an occasional tool to a continuous burden: and with serious consequences.

The family moment is dying, our friends are no longer friends, husbands and wives spend dinners together staring at their phones and we run our homes with virtual assistants. We fake our lives for the stage of social media. The life we lived for hundreds of thousands of years – from the Stone Age to Y2K – a life without the continuous presence of personal devices – is now at odds with reality.

And yet, occasionally, we get a glimpse of our previous life. Watching a show from the early 2000s is a surreal experience: students chatting in hallways, eating at restaurants or road trips driven in silence; all without a phone in sight. Everyone is available and present for each other.

We read about *The Lord of the Rings*, *A Song of Ice and Fire* – even *Harry Potter* – and we revel in the fantasy worlds they create; the simple pleasures of adventure without the presence of digital surveillance. We enjoy stories of slow living and fast action; of characters unburdened by the influence of digital media; of narratives with space to breathe in the ease of a tech free world.

Our favourite films take place without smartphones in the worlds of *Avatar*, *Titanic* and *Star Wars*. 9 out of the top 10 highest grossing films of all time are fantasy epics in the form of Marvel superhero movies, historical dramas and sci-fi.[39]

Our desire for nostalgia, as we saw in the *Introduction*, is directly related to our understanding that smartphones haven't made our lives easier, more enjoyable or more fulfilling: they've instead burdened us with more tasks, more stress and more responsibility.

We know the damage they've done, but we use them because everyone else does. We understand that society's moved to the Online: and we need to be part of it. The irony of a device which was supposed to make us more accessible, being contactable at any moment, has removed us from the physical environment in which we live.

Without a phone, conversation, interaction and awareness of others is normal. It's all there is. There's no intermediary, no anonymous person who may or may not be waiting on the other end of a Tweet. And yet, the ability for normal, human interaction is increasingly only available in fiction.

With no phone, our community is our community, society is society. Even the music on a car journey is a communal act; everyone can hear it, sing along or reflect in silence. Today, a kid playing "I Spy," counting Eddie Stobart lorries or asking, "Are we there yet?" seems impossible: just give them an iPad.

Our proximity to others meant that we were available for each other; to be engaged, to be interrupted, to be called upon. And, if we were alone, we could live with our own thoughts and contemplation. Today, we're determined to fill this silence with noise, even if it promises to be "relaxing," "calming," "meditative" or whatever. In the commercialisation of the quiet, there's an app for everything, even nothing. This has major implications.

Solitude

Today, wishing for peace and solitude is like asking someone to put their phone away at the cinema: difficult.

We live in a society in which privacy has been stolen from us; solitude, pried from us. And yet – even though

23

public space is littered with cameras – from CCTV to mobile phones – we should still have access to privacy and solitude when we're alone.

And yet, society demands we impose noise, distraction and surveillance on ourselves; not just through the presence of our phones but through virtual assistants, smart TVs and other devices (not to mention our self-surveillance on social media, fearing future reprisals of a yet-to-be unpopular opinion).

Our relationship with technology and its imposition on our lives has fundamentally changed.

Twenty years ago, a kid in the basement, on their computer all day, was seen as a kind of outcast. Today, it's all of us: and we're not limited to the basement. Our computer is with us all the time and we're not playing games: we're "living our lives."

If we asked the kid, "What are you doing down there?" and they said, "I'm living my life through a computer," we'd dismiss them as insane, take away the Cheezits and pull the plug.

And yet, this kid had a purpose: they were playing video games. That's all. They occupied a fantasy world – a world they, for better or worse, prioritised over the real one; but one which they, nevertheless, knew was a fantasy. This distinction has been largely destroyed.

Our technology is no longer a choice between access to information or entertainment: it's both.

Social media, online shopping – even search algorithms – would have us define ourselves by trends and categories, confining us to one idea, one style, one interest at a time. Our need to categorise and label suppresses growth, development and opportunity, limiting information and forcing us into neatly packaged, two dimensional users: and it's all accessible from our phones.

This reduction of the human being is exacerbated by digital entertainment – a snare for social discussion – limiting our unity to the latest TV show, football game or movie release. Instead of uniting on class lines, we instead unite around whether Bran should have been King.[40]

What we have in common is the lowest common denominator.

And the effects of this society – a society of individual suppression, cultural reduction and internet dependency – is a mental health crisis and the movement of society from a physical place to the ethereal realm of the Online.

When the Online drives our purpose in person, society-on-demand is, no longer, merely on demand: it's inescapable.

Time

The promise of the smartphone was to save time. Instead, they have *become* our time. As an invention to make our lives more efficient, they've succeeded in making life more complicated. The presence of our phones in all moments has made them synonymous with time itself.

And this is the fundamental problem of the smartphone: it has a watch. Our lived experience becomes inseparable from our awareness of time.

Today, when we check the time, we also check calls, messages, notifications and everything else. How can we treat time as a separate entity when, with each check of the clock, we are both checking out of society and into society-on-demand?

How many times have we taken out our phones to check the time and, just a few seconds later, put it back in our pockets, having forgotten to look? Our brains consider the phone itself as "content" to the point where its most basic functions are not just ignored: they're completely forgotten, even when we intend to use them. We check our phones so frequently that we forget what we checked them for. This is the habitual nature of the phone's relationship to us.

Growing up, I remember walking into rooms and forgetting what I went in for. This happened infrequently and, on the few occasions it did, I was able to enjoy the silent chuckle of my own stupidity. Today, we no longer walk into rooms and forget why we're there: today, our phones are the room.

Through our phones, we can dip in and out of rooms in seconds. We can visit the news room, the music room, the video room, the games room, not to mention pretty much anyone else's "room" we like, via social media.

And, as above, we're not going into these rooms, forgetting why we were there, a few times a year: We're going so often that we go without reason in the first place. We're unable to remember why we're there because there's literally no reason besides habit or, in many cases, addiction (more than one in three 18 to 30 year olds are addicted to their smartphones).[41]

Unsurprisingly, smartphones and their use have been a major cause of sleep deprivation, particularly in younger people. This is becoming endemic, with 29% of 6 to 10 year olds, 38% of 11 to 16 year olds and 57% of 17 to 23 year olds suffering from sleep problems at least three nights a week,[42] probably not helped by the 92% of 18 to 24 year olds using their phones in bed before going to sleep, nor the 74% if they wake up in the middle of the night.[43]

With smartphones increasingly used for generic TV consumption [44] and one in four children displaying problematic use, not to mention being over three times more likely to suffer depression, anxiety, stress, poor sleep and educational attainment:[45] the benefits of a smartphone outweighing its negatives – even if we ignored the other destructive behaviours it makes easier, such as pornography, gambling and social media – seems farfetched. Of course, adults can make their own decisions and control their use: but the problem (as with all addictive substances) is that exceptions prove the rule and, as things currently stand, the evidence is clear: compulsive use is the norm, not the exception: and it's getting worse.

When the majority of adults are addicted to their phones[46] and when the average 11 to 24 year old spends 2.5 hours a day on a computer, laptop or tablet, 2 hours a day watching TV and 3 hours on their phone:[47] we face a serious crisis, with devastating consequences for mental health, communication and social cohesion.

Part of this has been a major decline in literacy and reading for pleasure, with less than 1 in 3 children under the age of 18 reading daily outside of school, dropping to just over a quarter for those aged 14 to 16.[48]

At the risk of sounding predictable: it gets worse.

Literacy

In a survey of 40,000 children across the country, the National Literacy Trust found the most popular content for young people to read is texts, direct messages and in-game communications.[49]

This isn't simply a subversion of the "book" as a platform of communication, but the written word itself. That digital messages are the material of choice for roughly 90% of 8 to 18 year olds and with less than 1 in 3 reading on a daily basis,[50] there is – clearly – a crisis in literacy and the ability to focus, consume long form content or material of value.

One of the main consequences of society-on-demand is that children and young people are most exposed to its harms, following in the footsteps of their distracted and exhausted parents; their compulsive phone use and the escape of digital entertainment.

Not only are young people becoming more reliant on these devices, armed with the legitimisation and enablement of their parents: but class itself is becoming visible not just by clothes: but by *phones*.

While phones are the easiest option for stressed, overworked parents to distract their children, kids without distraction will be a sign of wealth; benefitting from parents with the time, energy and resources to occupy them (or with enough outdoor space for kids to occupy themselves).

Physical health is a major benefit of outdoor space, as well as improved social skills, resourcefulness and independence, leading to greater creativity and mental health.

Once again, it's the working class who suffer, this time from tools which are, supposedly, their liberation; achieved in the curation of an online persona: a paper ark in a flood of irrelevance. This is best exemplified by the Covid pandemic.

In the beginning, children showed an interest in the news, watching news briefings with their families. But this soon gave way to the usual disinterest in current events, preferring to scroll on their phones instead.

Ofcom's *Life in Lockdown* maps this decline, including comments from children as young as 12 such as, "I've never been into the news" and "I'm not really a news kind of person", to, "This is going to sound rude, but I just don't really care." These are symptomatic of a wider trend to disengage from reality. And, on the occasions kids do want to know what's going on, they tend to use social media (that beacon of accuracy!)[51]

The study identifies trends continuing from 2014, including "an increasing move towards short form content in the form of video snippets", consuming an increasing amount of content alone instead of with their families and the attempted emulation of YouTubers and TikTokkers through performing their own content in the knowledge it can be monetised, leading to a greater focus on self-image through the curation of social media and editing tools.

Another trend identified is the simultaneous use of multiple devices:

> *For example, Josie, 15, who every evening used her laptop to chat to her boyfriend via Skype, said she would typically be scrolling through her phone at the same time, looking at Instagram, Discord or TikTok.*[52]

According to Dialogues in Clinical Neuroscience, "Potential harmful effects of extensive screen time and technology use include heightened attention-deficit symptoms, impaired emotional and social intelligence, technology addiction, social isolation, impaired brain development, and disrupted sleep."[53]

In 2019, a study in *World Psychiatry* concluded the internet encourages "us to engage in attentional-switching and 'multi-tasking', rather than sustained focus,"[54] while a separate study in *PLOS One* found that even "when surfing the Internet, attentional scope is reduced, and this effect might continue after internet activity."[55]

Young people are toiling under the illusion that society-on-demand is not just important, but it's the only reality for their future. The persistent use of multiple devices and the constant need for distraction – not to mention the actual content they consume – is creating a socially impotent generation based on the trivialisation of physical reality and in person relationships and this, in turn, impacts the format of available content.

Just ten years ago, blogs were a large source of internet traffic. Over the past ten years, coinciding with the rise of social media, blogs have plummeted in popularity and readership. They have also – with some exceptions – become asinine; focused on "top 10s," "best things," and "five things you should never do on a cruise." These easily-digestible, get-in/get-out blogs are not only driven by Search Engine Optimisation, but by user demand. We've become accustomed to quick, easily digestible information, preferring our knowledge spoon fed. Many articles now contain "read times" at the beginning to assuage fears that it might take up a little bit of time and, yes, "We're sorry this isn't a video."

A recent survey of over 1,000 bloggers revealed that the most popular blog posts were "How-To guides" (76%) and "Lists" (54%), with the most effective blogging format being "Roundups." Additionally, blog posts with more images attained substantially better results.[56]

Consequently, the type of content we read has changed. The desire for long-form content or nuanced information is in decline. We've become utilitarian and market focused. Unsurprisingly, reading for pleasure is no longer a thing. The vast majority of content is boring: so why make it long?

And yet, there's a reason we turn to video to learn new things: it's even easier.

Writing in 2017, YouTube claimed "more than 7 out of 10 viewers often use YouTube to solve a problem when it comes to their job, studies or hobbies", and 86% said they often used YouTube to learn new things.[57] With 1.5 billion monthly users (this does not include users without a YouTube account), we can presume well over a billion people turned to YouTube to learn new skills or solve problems in 2017 alone.[58]

In 2020, YouTube became a major source of home-schooling, benefitting from increases in searches for skills like "cutting your own hair" and "how to" videos. Content with "for beginners" or "step by step" as search words increased by 65% year on year. Watch times for videos like guitar tutorials increased 40% and, for making Sourdough, 260%.[59] Clearly, much of this was pandemic induced; but the sheer volume of searches and increases in watch time, combined with the increased use of smartphones and time spent online, shows a decisive shift from text to video, even for education and informational purposes, with Gen Z preferring YouTube to printed books by 12%.[60]

But while videos may be easier, they're not necessarily more efficient, with YouTube functioning on ad-based models, filling videos with commercials and "Creators" taking to the end of the video to get to the point, just to increase watch time. And yet, the format is not the only problem...

In January 2022, an open letter was sent to YouTube's CEO, Susan Wojcicki, by The International Fact-Checking Network. The letter asked YouTube to "prevent disinformation and misinformation being weaponized against its users and society at large" through "unscrupulous actors" who "manipulate and exploit others".[61]

One major cause of this misinformation was YouTube's own recommendation algorithm, which accounted for "more than 70%" of viewing hours.[62]

The letter proposed four policies YouTube could implement to reduce these issues, including "providing context and offering debunks, clearly superimposed on videos or as additional video content", instead of YouTube's current "false dichotomy of deleting or not deleting content."[63]

Regulating free speech is often presented as an all or nothing task; either banned or completely unregulated. And this suits the narrative of Big Tech, empowered to hide behind "freedom" and "fairness", further prolonging the problem of misinformation.

Through the prevalence of smartphones, social media is replacing not just entertainment but our education, with a direct impact on literacy and concentration.

To return to the Literacy Trust, children with low reading engagement are more likely to consume what they're reading on screens,[64] an unsurprising fact given the lower quality, short form content and distractions included (advertisements, hyperlinks, images, etc). This impact cannot be overstated.

In 2020, a nursery in Oxfordshire found some of its kids returning from lockdown using American accents: a result of watching too much YouTube.[65]

And yet, in the face of rising phone use, particularly among young people, the government remains averse to doing anything about it. Instead, it plans to ensure even faster internet speeds across the country while, at the same time, trying to boost literacy.[66]

Of course, there's an easy way to boost literacy: reduce the use of mobile phones.

A 2015 study by LSE found that GCSE scores improved when mobile phones were banned from class,[67] with teachers drawing direct correlations between smartphones, media multi-tasking and concentration. As one teacher put it, "students, now, seem to find it particularly exhausting to read complex or long text without regular breaks. In the past, students seemed to be accustomed to attending to a text for a longer period of time".[68]

The triumph of short form content and the preference for digital entertainment over reading, combined with the distraction of smartphones and digital multi-tasking, was always going to impact academic performance.

If we continue to view our phones as more entertaining than books then it doesn't matter how much money the government throws at literacy: it won't work.

Instead, we need a fundamental reset in our perceptions and values.

As we've seen, a successful reset is precisely against the government's interests; interests which remain the same as Digital Entertainment: to quell, to placate, to distract. This is why literacy matters. Not because of an arbitrary reason to enjoy it: but because a life which relies solely on digital entertainment is a life that is subject to its content and objectives; to the realm of Big Tech and its interests; to acquiescence and the negation of our own thoughts and abilities; to be a passive consumer, not an active participant.

In our quest for more connectivity, these concerns are rarely considered. Instead, our need to escape has fuelled our desire for more content: and it's getting worse.

Speed

Given our insatiable consumption and the ubiquity of the smartphone, the only barriers we now face are cost and speed. Despite the availability of superfast broadband and 4G, for many, these advances aren't quick enough.

In this context, 5G makes sense. Significantly faster than 4G, 5G would enable almost immediate and, critically, simultaneous downloads of movies, music and TV shows, alongside a seamless browsing experience.

In an age of unlimited data, we're compelled to download as much as possible; delivering maximum choice for the assurance of oblivion; of erasing our surroundings and the hell of other people.

We're battered by content to the point where we no longer know what we want (if we knew in the first place). We have no idea which podcast we'll want to listen to, which vlog, live stream or movie we'll watch on our commute. And it doesn't matter. Instead, we can decide in the moment, with enough speed to watch, listen and consume whatever we want, whenever we want, and enough algorithmic power to suggest something of interest if we can't decide.

And yet, despite our plea for speed, 5G is potentially dangerous, compromising the safety of aircraft and affecting their ability to accurately measure the distance between the height of the plane and the runway beneath. This isn't a conspiracy.

Indeed, the threat is so severe that the CEOs of American Airlines, Delta and United, as well as the head of the Federal Aviation Administration, among others, wrote to the US Transport Secretary, claiming 5G required "immediate intervention ... to avoid significant operational disruption to air passengers, shippers, supply chain and delivery of needed medical supplies."[69]

Airbus and Boeing expressed similar concerns as recently as January 2022, with British Airways, Japan Airlines, All Nippon and others suspending all Boeing 777 flights to the US due to 5G safety concerns.[70]

President Biden even had to ask 5G providers to hold-off on roll-out "and abide by what was being requested by the airlines".[71]

The idea that 5G, while safe for most purposes,[72] should compromise something as essential as travel while – at the same time – offering little value to our needs as a society, is absurd, and another example of improvement for improvement's sake, even when it threatens critical infrastructure.

But despite planes smashing into runways, there is, potentially, a bigger problem: its impact on phone use.

When 4G launched, it changed the way we consumed. Users with 4G used their phones significantly more than those without it for even basic activities, including watching TV (57% vs 40%) and instant messaging (63% to 50%).[73]

Critically, the introduction of 4G and superfast broadband coincided with the closure of hundreds of playgrounds across the country in the wake of austerity, further cementing a switch from physical society to society-on-demand.[74] [75]

The closure of playgrounds represents the damage of austerity and the impact of shrinking public space; with serious mental health consequences for children, in particular, with physical, outdoor activity replaced by digital entertainment.

According to the *Royal College of Paediatrics and Child Health*, 41% of 11 to 24 year olds said screen time had affected their play or fun, with 35% saying it had a negative effect on their mood or mental health.[76]

A recent report by *The National Trust* found that:

Until quite recently, if a child was sent to their bedroom during daylight hours, it was because they had been behaving badly.

Today, things are very different. The average child's bedroom is no longer a place of punishment, but an entertainment hub: the epicentre of their social lives. Here they can access the outside world via their mobile phone, TV or computer screen; or immerse themselves in a beguiling fantasy world of computer games, whose scenarios are so convincing that children sometimes have difficulty distinguishing between this 'virtual reality' and the real world. Why would they ever need to venture outdoors again?[77]

Biologist Robert Pyle referred to this as "the extinction of experience",[78] an obvious result of what *The National Trust* calls "Nature Deficit Disorder", a phrase originally coined by journalist Richard Louv to describe "the human costs of alienation from nature, among them: diminished use of the senses, attention difficulties, and higher rates of physical and emotional illnesses."[79]

Besides public space, the home itself is shrinking in available space, with childrens' "radius of activity" – the area around the home where children are "allowed to roam unsupervised" – declining by almost 90% since the 1970s.[80]

In a disastrous coincidence, the reduction of physical space through austerity arrived at the same time as the expansion of the Online, laying the groundwork for the future direction of society – a society of increasing alienation – building the infrastructure of society-on-demand while, at the same time, destroying the infrastructure of physical society.

As usual, the government's response has been to accelerate the problem; with increasing digitisation, greater screen use and time spent online: another cycle of cause and effect where the shrinking of physical space – in public and in private – has driven people further online; itself causing a further reduction in public space and the perceived need for less private space (an issue compounded by the housing crisis in supply, quality and affordability).

And so, if 5G has anywhere near as significant an impact on phone use: smartphone addiction can be expected to rise well beyond current levels and public space will continue to decline, aided by the placation of our devices. The consequence of an internet 10 times faster than 4G, with greater connectivity between devices, will do nothing to stem our increasing levels of addiction and distraction.

Today, UK adults spent nearly four times as long online via smartphones than they do on computers, with Ofcom referring to the smartphone as the new "base layer of connectivity".[81]

Given that smartphones are the platform upon which our obstacles are most actively engaged and, given their ubiquity in each moment of our lives, even when we're asleep (70% of Gen Z and Millennials sleep with their phones within arm's reach, and more than half check their phone when they wake up in the middle of the night),[82] our lives become journeys without place and time, never "on," never "off," like the skip between tracks or the black between channels: a switch without a click, between everything and nothing.

And so we live our lives never fully appreciating – nor truly being – anywhere. Whether that's at the cinema, watching TV, travelling, having dinner, going for a walk – even going to sleep – we are never really *here*. And that means society, too, is never really here. Instead, society is replaced by society-on-demand; a society not simply "on-demand" when we want it, but which remains active whether we want it to or not: our knowledge of its existence and fear of missing out maintains its threat of relevance to the physical society in which we live.

Under fascist regimes, banning books was a logical policy: control what people read, suppress information, entrench ignorance and deprive them of hope and alternative ideas, and ruling elites gain a better grip on power and an easier way to implement their agenda.

Today, there's no need. Banning books would make almost no difference. Instead, governments can act under the guise of personal empowerment and individual liberation through the rule of personal devices.

Instead of banning things, governments can, instead, *add* things. When something is banned, questions are asked. If it's banned, why is it banned? What does the government not want me to know? Why am I not allowed to read this?

And yet, if more is introduced – if things are, instead, added – what the government prefers banned can die a silent death, replaced by something not just innocuous, but positively encouraged.

Banning young people from voting, for example, doesn't need to happen: just give them a phone and a Netflix account.

The impact of austerity, the decline of public space and – critically – the preference for society-on-demand and the Online, enabled by the smartphone, is serious.

Even in public, people are glued to their screens, absorbed in their headphones, divorced from everyone else. For the few that aren't, they're anxious even in company; unable to make eye contact, glancing at the floor – eyes darting sideways – begging for a distraction: and the phone in their pocket is a reliable saviour.

Efficiency for Deficiency's Sake

It's been fifteen years since Apple launched the iPhone.

Since then, a fundamental shift in society – of a present, physically-engaged population to absent, digitally-enslaved individuals – has changed who we are and how we live.

Technology, with its presumption of progress and intrinsic benefit, has reaped the rewards of a system incapable of challenging itself; refusing to assess the impact of new products, systems and services.

We presume that any attempt to improve efficiency and shorten tasks is inherently good. And yet, its impact is rarely addressed.

For something to become quicker, something needs to take longer. Instead of using our time to do less, we're encouraged to do more; to buy more stuff or waste away in front of a screen (preferably both).

Consequently, despite using these products to save time, we find ourselves with less; absorbing content on the same "time-saving" devices in the form of social media, online shopping, digital entertainment, etc.

The myth of efficiency has built an economy based on distraction rather than utility.

And while the smartphone may be an unpopular choice for this attack, perhaps a better, universally-loathed example, is required: the automated phone menu.

You know how it goes. Whether it's an airline, broadband provider or doctor's surgery, navigating the menu before an eternity on hold – only to be cut off without a call back – is infuriating. And yet, this process was designed for efficiency; removing the hassle of another human being and, instead, allowing robots to present a limited set of useless options.

But this time-wasting, violence-inducing process is fundamental to the way "efficiency" works: it's deficient by design.

Like other forms of automation in the replacement of human beings, we're treated like the robots we're forced to interact with.

Press 1 for something else.

Press 2 for imminent phone break.

The prioritisation of profit and efficiency through limited options and one-way dictation has resulted in absolute deficiency, depriving us of the conversation and support required. And who do we have to thank for this? Michael J. Freeman.

His first creation was a 200-pound robot teacher, programmed to simulate "infinite patience", [83] an irony which clearly escaped his notice, with the automated phone menu.

We live in a world where anyone can patent their invention without the slightest consideration of wider consequence; a world where – from one person's idea – monumental damage is achieved, fundamentally changing the way society operates and the way we interact with each other.[84]

Of course, it wasn't just Michael J. Freeman. It was Bill Gates, Mark Zuckerberg, Jack Dorsey, Steve Jobs,

Zhang Yiming, Larry Page, Elon Musk and Jeff Bezos, to name a few.

These guys (all of them, *guys*) invented, patented and presided over major technological "advances" on the promise that their products and services would improve our lives. The smartphone's no exception.

When Big Tech "follows its dreams with mind and heart" it is not, as Disney believed, "a dream come true for you and me." It is, mostly, a disaster.

-

So far, we've seen the damage smartphones have caused to our mental health, relationships, our ability to focus, literacy rates, time and public space.

And yet, the recognition that these products cause immense damage is not, as we might suspect, limited to its opponents. Steve Jobs, Bill Gates, Google's Sundar Pichai and Snapchat's Evan Spiegel seem to have analysed the downsides of these products for themselves, limiting screen time for their own children. Steve Jobs banned iPads, Pichai and Gates refused their kids cell phones and Spiegel limits his kids to just an hour and half's screen time a week.[85] Even Mark Zuckerberg was opposed to his own children "sitting in front of a TV or a computer for a long period of time."[86]

Of course, Facebook has no problem prioritising its own interests over the public good.[87] Apple still creates highly addictive devices, Google continues to monopolise the web through ad-driven search and Snapchat remains one of the most popular apps for young people.[88] The idea that these products are "bad for my kids but fine for everyone else" is exactly the kind of hypocrisy required of a world that's deeply unequal; a sink or swim society where compassion extends only to our selves and our immediate families; where staying afloat requires others to drown.

What's the solution?

The problems in our society are, as always, political. And yet, as we've seen, their solutions are, firstly, technological, as we untangle ourselves from the web of society-on-demand. This requires a technological regression – a repurposing – of its systems and features.

The political battles we face remain insignificant compared to the war on our time, mental health and physical presence.

The smartphone is the basis – the foundational object – of society-on-demand. Without it, the obstacles of social media, pornography, football, TV and on-demand streaming would not be anywhere near as challenging – accessible in a specific time and place – versus the ubiquity of the smartphone. The smartphone's continuous presence, its ease of access and compulsive use elevates these obstacles from occasional to perennial.

Its disproportionate effects on Gen Z and Gen Alpha have empowered the proliferation of short form content, the decline of literacy, the shortening of attention spans, the decline of public space and a mental health crisis; all of which serve to reinforce its relevance in our lives as both the means of our escape and our desire to do so.

Having established the smartphone as the gateway to our problems, we can now assess the specific issues it platforms; the major players in society-on-demand and the impact they've had on our relationships, mental health and physical society: the obstacles to our humanity and wider political change.

SOCIAL MEDIA

Social media is where society dies.

It segregates our interests and aggregates our time. A place where information – and facts – are managed on our behalf: where we all become reflectors of the Zuckerberg-Dorsey machine; relegated to a handful of interests, feelings and opinions: where the three-dimensional human becomes a 2D relic.

Social media, as a fundamental component of society-on-demand, is changing what society is and how it operates.

According to Sean Parker, the founding President of Facebook: social media "literally changes your relationship with society, with each other ... It probably interferes with productivity in weird ways. God only knows what it's doing to our children's brains."[89]

Designed to be addictive through continuous dopamine hits, we re-enter these platforms to alleviate our withdrawals.

As Parker explains:

> *The thought process that went into building these applications, Facebook being the first of them, ... was all about: 'How do we consume as much of your time and conscious attention as possible?' And that means that we need to sort of give you a little dopamine hit every once in a while, because someone liked or commented on a photo or a post or whatever. And that's going to get you to contribute more content, and that's going to get you ... more likes and comments. It's a social-validation feedback loop ... exactly the kind of thing that a hacker like myself would come up with, because you're exploiting a vulnerability in human psychology. The inventors, creators — it's me, it's Mark [Zuckerberg], it's Kevin Systrom on Instagram, it's all of these people — understood this consciously. And we did it anyway.*[90]

Parker isn't alone.

Chamath Palihapitiya, former Vice President for User Growth at Facebook, claims social media has "created tools that are ripping apart the social fabric of how society works", with "no civil discourse, no cooperation; misinformation, mistruth."[91]

Frances Haugen, former product lead for Civic Misinformation and then Counter-Espionage, claims Facebook is "a company with control over our deepest thoughts, feelings and behaviors", needing "real oversight."

Tristan Harris, a former product manager at Google, put it this way in the CBS documentary, *Brainhacking*:

> *The game is getting attention at all costs. And the problem is it becomes this race to the bottom of the brainstem, where if I go lower on the brainstem to get you, you know, using my product, I win. But it doesn't end up in the world we want to live in. We don't end up feeling good about how we're using all this stuff.* [92]

Asked if Silicon Valley is programming apps or people, Harris responds that "inadvertently, whether they want to or not, they are shaping the thoughts and feelings and actions of people. They are programming people. There's always this narrative that technology's neutral. And it's up to us to choose how we use it. This is just not true."[93]

Not to be outdone, *Brainhacking* also interviewed a neuroscientist, a psychologist and a Big Tech designer, all of whom agreed social media was the cause of serious behavioural and mental health issues and that the companies behind these technologies have knowingly created products to encourage compulsive use. Politics and mental health are seen as neutral ground, used whatever way necessary to fertilise user engagement.

Ramsay Brown, a computer programmer and neuroscientist, created an app which imposed a 12 second delay when opening social media, providing the user with a moment of calm before use. He approached Apple to sell it on the App Store but was rejected on the grounds that it would encourage us to spend less time on our phones.[94]

Meanwhile, in February 2022, the App Store launched Donald Trump's "Truth Social",[95] a platform with over $1 billion, enabling the political Right.

Society-on-demand requires our attention. And the best way to achieve this is to create the illusion that we're missing out; that to not be on these platforms is to forego our ability to not just stay up to date, but to progress in our own lives; a place we're encouraged to share our thoughts, opinions, beliefs and "work", to build our own "communities" and "followings."

Refusal is death.

Today, those without a social media account are considered pariahs or professional failures. No LinkedIn, no ambition. No WhatsApp, no friends.

Just as Parker, Harris and Palihapitiya revealed the addictive qualities of these programmes, we've spent the past ten years proving them right; living for the Retweet, the share, the like, the comment, the follower, the subscriber. And, when we engage online, it's often for the purpose of boosting our own presence; worshipping at the idols of others while demanding they build statues of us.

And yet, as more evidence emerges of the damage social media causes and the way these companies behave, we continue to use it, complaining about these platforms on the same platforms we're complaining about.

Why?

Because we believe in its promise: the promise that social media offers the best way to be seen, to be heard; to be understood: the best way to express ourselves, to succeed, to remember: to connect. In short, we rely on social media because it has a monopoly on Relationship and, through this, has fundamentally changed what a relationship is...

The Myth of Exposure

Today, a relationship is "Follower" to "Influencer," "Subscriber" to "Creator," "Poster" to "Scroller;" relationships based on the pursuit of exposure.

If we want to be seen, we're told to use the biggest platforms, increasing our chance of being noticed. We want to interact with others and yet – on social media – people are not people at all: they're users, followers, likers, commenters. Anything but real human beings.

Of course, we could launch our own websites, but this requires money, time, knowledge and, most of all: patience.

Facebook, Instagram, TikTok, YouTube, Snapchat and others already possess an established framework and, consequently, millions of users. All we need is an account. And with a business model like that, why wouldn't we use it? Ease of use and the promise of influence outweigh our concerns for privacy and meaning.

Social media changes the way we perceive the world, providing the delusion that the more we use it, the more we achieve.

We allow ourselves to revel in our own "success," believing that because we've Tweeted, posted on Facebook, uploaded on TikTok or signed a petition, we've "done our bit." No need for anything else.

This glorification of the self through the prioritisation of the Online allows us to disengage; refusing struggle and meaningful engagement; comforted by the delusion that what we do online matters just as much – if not more – as what we do in person.

We believe it because we believe engagement is proof of its relevance: that hundreds of millions of people can't be wrong. Given that our friends and family are on social media; given that journalists and newspapers, actors and TV stars, football players and, seemingly, the rest of the world, participates in social media, it is – clearly – the best place to connect, share an opinion, or whatever else. We believe our ability to change things, politically or otherwise, resides on these platforms.

We've heard it said: "Use the internet to make your arguments and change minds, where your audience is, potentially, millions. Or keep your opinions to yourself and those around you, for limited reach." This argument supposes two things.

First, that our ability to post something online will be read by more people than we could speak to in person and, second, that anyone who sees this post will, a. care and, b. change their mind. The most likely result is that they will either, a. already agree and, therefore, don't need to see it or, b. don't agree and, now they've seen it, can respond to tell us how stupid we are.

What we share on the internet rarely results in a changing of minds because, increasingly, what we post is offensive or belligerent (something we believe is increasingly necessary to "get noticed.") We're not interested in listening to each other or discussing ideas and, even if we wanted to, there's no ability to engage in real time. Meaningful conversation is impossible. Social media either placates people or radicalises them, making us either impotent or dangerous. We're incentivised to oppose.

Of course, some platforms have live video, allowing (in theory) real-time, meaningful engagement. But what is "engagement?" Comments reflecting a need to be noticed through platitudes of abuse or hyperbolic agreement. The comment box, live chat and reply buttons are not there to facilitate meaningful engagement but to boost the "Creator's" engagement stats. These platforms claim to enable discussion, yet their algorithms peddle division, selling the delusion of progress with emoji-induced agreement. The provision of an interaction facility – a live chat, comment, reply, like, etc. – is nothing more than a facade to juice views and fund ads. The truth is, if exposure was guaranteed regardless of engagement, we wouldn't speak to anyone else because we'd rather agree with ourselves, living a life unchallenged in a perverse, dopamine death loop.

Opinion First, Human Never

Intolerance and abuse are accelerating because the immediacy of these platforms promotes a rash and irrational response. Combine this with the ease of engagement through society-on-demand, the continuous presence of entertainment and the presentation of everything as immediate and knowable, and we have an environment in which it's reasonable to demand and expect immediate solutions to the problems we face.

The danger here isn't that we *want* immediate solutions: it's that immediate solutions are a fantasy. Instead of acknowledging the need to work for change, to exert effort through nuanced platforms of communication, to convince others from a default position of respect and good will and to provide each other with the benefit of the doubt; we instead demand our problems are solved as easily as it is to express them in the first place; allowing us to see the act of commenting as an action in itself, sufficient for the changes we need; and this makes discussion itself a source of entertainment.

Of course, if discussion was not entertaining, we'd be inclined to avoid it. Genuine human engagement and conversation *should* be entertaining. It's a natural source of focus and progress; inherently rewarding; bringing us closer together. But when our engagement is little more than a performance for increased viewership; to find a winner and a loser; to be noticed and idolised rather than seek meaningful change: it reduces interaction to competition; the first step to reducing each other – and ourselves – to pieces of content: the 2D relic.

When everyone is reduced to an opinion, when there's no recourse for meaningful discussion; we become defined *as* opinions, not people *with* opinions. The humanity of who we are; our experiences, character and everything else, not to mention other opinions we might possess or actions we may or may have not taken; is removed from the equation. And, once humanity is removed, we're empowered to be militant, not nuanced; envious, not selfless; rash, not patient. We're empowered to do nothing less than reject others wholesale; a resounding "No" to an entire person.

When we do this, not only do we reject the value of another human being; but we make it impossible to engage. We can't convince others or share our opinion because we've made it clear we reject them for theirs. We have no interest in speaking unless it's to tell them how wrong they are and, if we can do so with some abuse for a few more Likes, all the better.

When we're conditioned through social media and society-on-demand in general, through poor communication and false standards: we're going to have massive problems. And that's exactly what we're seeing.

Not only is the Left less able to convince, it's also completely disinterested in doing so; further separating itself from meaningful discussion and isolating itself from others, making it almost impossible to establish new networks of friends and, instead, forging new enemies.

The idea that certain opinions are beyond the pale of human redemption, or even basic change – combined with the practical approach of campaigning via social media and building solidarity predominantly online – is why the Left continues to fail. Yes, there's a clear difference in resources between Left and Right and, of course, the Left is fighting against a dominant and pervasive Right-wing narrative. But none of this is going to change if the Left continues to condemn, not convince; to glory in its own self-righteousness.

Online, conversation is commentary: two or more people trying to make their voices heard. Worse still, it's happening in front of an audience they're not even sure exists. All they know is that this audience *may* exist; either right now, in five minutes, tomorrow or the next day.

The "conversation" is on display, available for people to see whenever and, increasingly, wherever. This cannot be a normal conversation because it's a conversation under surveillance and an engagement each "side" wants to win. A conversation like this isn't a conversation: it's a performance. Once we remove privacy and impose competition; conversation – genuine, human interaction – dies. There's a prevention of nuance. A dereliction of new ideas. Controversial questions cannot be asked, nor opinions tolerated, because both sides of the debate are absolute: and there's an audience to win. There's no room for common ground because everyone's polarised. No one dares understand each other because doing so would mean we had something in common; that we were prepared to agree on some level or, even worse, see our enemies as human.

During an in-person meeting, we can discuss, debate – even argue – and feel closer because of it. We can emerge, for better or worse, better understood and with a greater understanding of others.

The adage of "keep your friends close and your enemies closer" is not so much a piece of advice as something that happens when we engage with our enemies. Our "enemies" *do* become closer because we can see them (in most cases) as fellow strugglers: as human beings.

The levels of intolerance we're currently witnessing – and committing – is not normal. When social media promotes reactionary engagement on both sides, it's clear that our efforts are misplaced. As we've seen, the nature of these platforms promotes division and, therefore, even if we wished to engage in a meaningful way, we'd find ourselves unable to do so. The idea that 280 characters of public "debate" is a good way to make progress is, clearly, delusional: but it's a delusion we've all fallen for.

So what's the solution?

It's unreasonable to have *no* place for online discussion. It's also not sensible. As we've seen, the internet is not, in itself, a terrible place. We're just too stupid to use it sensibly.

One way to elevate meaning and rehumanise our engagement with others is to restore a basic level of inefficiency.

The immediacy of these platforms and their ease of use is, as we've seen, a key feature of society-on-demand, particularly through social media. This makes it all too easy to speak without thinking, which is then magnified through algorithms promoting reactionary, emotionally charged content to provoke a hyperbolic response.

When we compare this to the pre-internet era, the differences are stark.

A hundred years ago, if we couldn't speak in person, we either couldn't speak at all, or we wrote letters.

Letters took time.

They took time to send, deliver, read and, consequently, *they took time to write.*

Letters either facilitated a meeting in person or sufficed as their own form of communication. As their own form of communication, wasting time and resources writing short, frivolous notes would have been ludicrous.

Instead, letters were formulated to express everything a normal conversation might confer; desire and concern, an update on recent events, plans for the future, etc. Their contents were purposeful and, importantly: considered. Because this process took time, it was important that everything which needed to be said was done clearly, with room for the recipient to understand and respond.

Even our own handwriting allowed the recipient to attain a sense of how we were feeling at the time: more ink here, harder press there, quick movement here, firm stop there.

And, while the telephone did not provide as much inefficiency or opportunity to consider our words, we were able to get closer to a physical, in person discussion; allowing us to communicate in real time with most of the nuance available in physical conversation, improving on the clues offered by the stroke of a pen, with a clearer set of idiosyncrasies and inflexions.

Computers reject both of these. They deny graphology. They detest nuance. Text on a screen tells us nothing about how fast we typed or how hard we hit keys, nor the length of time between each stroke or the number of times we hit delete. These are important indicators of our emotional state; something the pen and the telephone provide but is denied entirely by digital technology (unless you want to use a stylus. Ew).

Comparing a letter to an e-mail is like comparing different languages, not least because we can delete and retype in real time, requiring less planning, thought and consideration. When writing a letter, we'd have to start all over again if we made a mistake, which is why letters were often planned before they were written, taking longer to write as we considered our next words carefully.

Inefficiency benefited both Writer and Responder, with plenty of opportunities to destroy their letters even after they were penned. Today, a quick Tweet and the damage is done.

And yet, for all its faults, e-mail is certainly better than what followed...

Social media invited the prolific use of direct messaging, cementing bite-sized content as our preferred means of communication.

We're now so used to speaking via DM that messages are no longer conversations at all: they're cries for attention.

A DM is a prevention of conversation by default. Its very nature is to demand a "conversation" within the app itself. Why is this a problem? Because these apps are designed to function as content and entertainment; to ensure the user is continuously checking their phone. The best way to do this is to break conversation into bite-sized messages, providing emojis and gifs in the absence self-expression. "Hey, how's it going?" becomes an hour-long series of conversational snippets, adding nothing to how a real time conversation might unfold via phone call, or even the meaningful outcome of a carefully considered letter, to which we would not expect an immediate response (and would, therefore, contain significantly more value, as above).

Texts are so common that we've forgotten what they were for in the first place. Originally designed to *arrange* phone calls or meetings, they've now replaced them.

Twenty years ago, texting was a painful process. It made no sense to hold a conversation this way. Three taps for "c," *pause,* one tap for "a," *pause*, three taps for "l," *pause*, three taps for "l" again, *pause* – by the time you got to the space function, you might as well have called them to phone you back.

Clearly, texts were not meant to be used as a conversation replacement and yet, thanks to social media and the smartphone, this is exactly what they've become.

Today, apps like WhatsApp, Snapchat and Twitter have broken conversation into mini pieces of content. With a keyboard of individual letters, it's much easier to write for long periods of time – and quickly.

Gifs, memes and emojis have replaced our vocabulary. We now communicate in feelings, unable to express ourselves in text because we're no longer used to reading or writing anything longer than a couple of sentences. It's far easier to allow Chuck Norris or Peter Griffin to do it for us.

Our devices have prioritised efficiency and, in doing so, have destroyed not just consideration, but conversation itself.

A quick solution might be to make all direct messaging apps revert to the traditional phone pad, rather than individually lettered keys; requiring the user to type slowly, pressing numbers several times to get the letters they want. This would incentivise phone calls and in person meetings over DMs, reducing the impact of content-driven-messaging.

Restoring Tolerance

In US comedy show *Curb Your Enthusiasm*, the audience follows a satirised version of Larry David, creator of *Seinfeld*. The show is a largely improvised commentary on a society that's lost all sense of etiquette; a restaurant putting "ugly" people at the back and "pretty" people at the front, or the refusal to divulge personal information, jeopardising flight safety, etc.

The show is best viewed as a collection of fictionalised social experiments in a hyperbolic version of everyday life. As such, the main source of comedy stems from the tension between Larry and those he encounters in nonsensical, social difficulties, and his refusal to let things slide, choosing confrontation over submission.

Of course, these confrontations often lead to a heated exchange, with Larry screaming, "Fuck you and I'll see you tomorrow!"[96]

And this is the reaction we've lost.

To be clear, I don't think screaming, "Fuck you and I'll see you tomorrow" is a good idea, but it is – ironically – emblematic of a functional society; a society where problems are confronted, even if the injustice of the original offence persists. Larry knows he'll see them the next day, that he may well need them on other occasions, and so a relationship has to be maintained, even if it's mutually loathed.

In the show, there's a noticeable lack of social media and smartphones (we only really see the use of phones for calls and texts), maintaining the audience's focus on the physical society the characters are forced to endure.

And so, far from being a statement of an irreparable, broken society; "Fuck you and I'll see you tomorrow" is an affirmation. It affirms that, yes, "Fuck you": but I know I have to see you tomorrow and I know I have to deal with this and we'll have to speak again.

And, so long as that's the case – so long as we refuse the retreat, the escape – the surrender – of society-on-demand: things can improve, relationships can be established and society will become stronger.

Online, the power of our disagreements and antagonisms ties us in an emotional web of necessity; unable to function without the pain, angst and passion of mutual loathing. Our struggle becomes our motivation. Our pain becomes a requirement. We build cathedrals of factionalism, refusing to engage with those we disagree with (or who disagree with us).

We can "block," "mute," mock or campaign for their destruction and, most easily of all, campaign for a kind of online boycott (after abusing them first).

We treat the Online as a colosseum where our most savage abuse and factional put-downs are blasted into cyberspace, masked as morality and social justice, to cheers of an already agreeable audience. The mask of our morality is to magnify our own voice. We don't care if we bring anyone with us. In fact, we'd rather we didn't. Convincing someone means we have to get dirty: and we'd rather be clean. We don't believe in redemption because redemption is for those who are already dead – socially or otherwise. Apologies are cheap. Change is impossible. We strive for an image of perfection, an image beyond reproach: but the goalposts are always moving.

We double-down on difference and pledge our allegiance to the fracturing of relationships; a splinter-society in a self-righteous sling.

Our devotion to division is a function for the triumph of emotion over critical thinking, feeling over humility, fragility over respect.

Social media has convinced us that consumption is the same as participation; that scrolling, liking and commenting and sharing are the same as progressing our own lives and meaningful change.

Today, emotions lead our thoughts because social media – and web design in general – is designed to evoke a visceral response; a polarised express of emotion on rails of self-promotion.

Political Implications

Of course, social media isn't *all* bad. Progressive causes are championed through YouTube and Twitter, in particular, as places to share, analyse and discuss; even to promote upcoming events. And yet, these are not purely progressive platforms.

As one Facebook Executive told *Politico* in September 2020: "Right-wing populism is always more engaging," which is why the algorithm favours right-wing content.[97]

Just a year later, this statement looks dismissive at best, with former Facebook employee, Frances Haugen, unveiling internal evidence suggesting the algorithm itself "can veer people interested in conservative topics into radical or polarizing ideas and groups/pages."[98] And it doesn't end here.

In a US Senate hearing, Haugen confirmed Facebook prioritised its own profits over user safety, resulting in "a system that amplifies division, extremism, and polarization — and undermining societies around the world." Haugen continued: "In some cases, this dangerous online talk has led to actual violence that harms and even kills people. In other cases, their profit optimizing machine is generating self-harm and self-hate — especially for vulnerable groups, like teenage girls. These problems have been confirmed repeatedly by Facebook's own internal research."[99] But it's not just Facebook.

An internal study for Twitter found that "the mainstream political right enjoys higher algorithmic amplification than the mainstream political left. Consistent with this overall trend, our second set of findings studying the U.S. media landscape revealed that algorithmic amplification favours right-leaning news sources."[100]

And yet, there are enough examples of social media enabling justice and support for people who would, without social media, be overlooked. Twitter's importance for citizen journalism, for people to share their assaults or experiences and achieve subsequent police investigations, as happened with journalist Owen Jones,[101] or in sharing information and promoting certain causes, is obvious.

There's no doubt that without social media, the mainstream press would continue to remain largely unchallenged. And yet, *with* social media, not only does the Right have the mainstream press, amplified through its own social media channels (and, because of their already dominant position, is better represented on social media), but the Right also benefits from right-wing influencers, ordinary people and other organisations.

There is no way in which the Left – even with a large social media presence – is able to compete with the mainstream media, the right-wing press, right-wing social media and the algorithms which amplify these voices. The Left is under-represented by four to one.

And yet, we remain convinced that social media is a necessity, able to advance the Left over the Right; to shift society in the direction of dignity and justice. Instead, the rise of Trump, Johnson, Duterte, Bolsonaro, Modi and others seems to have given us no pause for thought, buying into the myth of these platforms when most evidence points to the Left swimming against a tidal wave of ignorance and hate.

Hashtag activism exemplifies our desire to help others: but it also demonstrates our exasperation with physical reality, believing a post on social media – a platform controlled by algorithms favouring the Right and dominated by non-progressive voices – is going to do anything to affect the outcome of a particular physical circumstance. We've become desperate, trusting in "the democratisation of the media" without considering how (and how not) to use it.

We want to help others so badly – to do *something* – that we delude ourselves into thinking a Tweet is going to achieve this, whether it's to #savebritney or #saverayan.

The truth, of course, is that Britney was always going to win her case: she was Britney Spears and, consequently, benefitted from immense public pressure – protests on the streets and favourable media coverage – which did not, in any way, require the use of hashtags. Rayan, a five year old boy who died after falling down a well, was always going to receive the care, effort and support of those involved in his rescue, including the dozens of people working day and night to free him, in addition to the hundreds of locals camped nearby, praying for his life, in physical solidarity with him and each other.[102]

But this wasn't the first time a child became trapped in a well for days. In 1987, Jessica McClure, just 18 months old, fell into a well and became stuck 22 ft. beneath the surface. Dozens of rescue workers were called in and, 58 hours later, she was freed. The event was broadcast across the United States, with millions hoping for her release; a world without the internet, social media and, for the vast majority of people, a world even without a mobile phone. And yet, despite their absence, the town of Midland, Texas, was able to save her.[103]

The fire brigade doesn't answer to a hashtag. Nor an ambulance to a Facebook post. These services exist in person, fulfilling their function to serve society without the need for a Tweet to validate their existence. Of course, these organisations are not infallible, but they are here – and their chance of success is not determined or aided by how loudly we campaign on social media.

All of which points to the simple and depressing fact that we no longer trust in our physical institutions because we no longer trust in others. We believe our football team has a better chance of winning if we scream at the TV. We believe our gratitude is real only when we talk about it on TikTok. We believe our food – our entire lifestyle – is only real when we post a photo on Instagram. We've become so disillusioned with society that we've lost faith in its ability to function without our own involvement.

And yet, if we spend our time campaigning on social media – achieving incredibly limited results, at best – then we're not spending time campaigning or building solidarity or protesting in physical society. The government doesn't care if we campaign on social media. They care if we campaign in public: if we occupy physical space.

The Arab Spring succeeded because Twitter was used to organise in person campaigns: it was not a campaign tool within itself. Instead, information shared online translated to in person protest. Likewise, Extinction Rebellion and Just Stop Oil have used online campaigns to share information, converting this knowledge to in person campaigns.

And yet, beyond their success, we need to consider the disasters ennobled by social media: empowering Duterte in the Philippines through Twitter "Influencers",[104] the incitement of violence for the Capitol riots on January 6th (not forgetting Trump's initial election in 2016 with the help of Cambridge Analytica), [105] anti-vax conspiracy theorists, the failure to elect the Labour Party in 2017 and 2019 (revealing its limitations) and, instead, impose a right-wing populist in Boris Johnson, etc.

To view social media as an indisputable, net benefit for progressive organisation is only possible because of the implicit division within it; that we easily forget the success of other causes because we're so consumed with our own, talking to ourselves, with people who already agree with us.

The sooner we accept this – that not only is social media extremely damaging to our mental health, our relationships and attention spans, but also to progressive causes – the sooner we can strategize to better use our resources, empowering a healthier, more human and effective strategy for change.

When everything is ultra-charged and ultra-accessible, compounded by reduced attention spans and a need for instant gratification; our reliance on speed and convenience only serves to empower society-on-demand, where we can engage with anything at whatever time we want. Normal society – physical, in person society – is too inconvenient, too difficult and too disappointing. And yet, as we've seen, this becomes self-fulfilling; enslaved to society online through our phones; agitating, distracting and influencing us in the physical world and, finally, convincing us that a life on social media is as meaningful as real-world events.

The problem with social media isn't just that it's run for the wrong reasons, that the wrong things are shown (and not shown), that it's addictive and damages our personal – as well as social – lives. The problem is that it takes our natural insecurities – to be heard, to be known, to be appreciated – and elevates them beyond in person relationships and society; beyond communication, knowledge and appreciation.

Society becomes not something in our immediate vicinity – something we interact with on a daily basis – where we live, work, visit or spend time together; but something immeasurably bigger: a society that is nowhere yet, somehow, everywhere. A society which is always accessible, no matter where we are; where our physical location is influenced and controlled by the ever present society-on-demand. Every coffee shop, restaurant and hotel has an account to be "tagged," every product a hashtag to be shared, every activity, experience and relationship a photo, video or comment to be seen and replied to.

But a society that's always accessible is a society which is also completely inaccessible to most things, for most people. A society where all things exist means *what* we access has to be chosen. We cannot stay active in a gardening "community," a fashion "community," a football "community" and a music "community" when each community demands and expects continuous engagement and consumption, and when algorithms seek to divide us even more, reducing us to one community at a time.

But a society in person – actual, physical society – expects limited engagement. It expects us to be focused on one activity, one person or one group at a time – and for a set period of time: gardening for an hour, football for 90 minutes or jamming in your basement for an evening with friends (driving the neighbours crazy who are now, fortuitously, forced to accept that they, too, live in a physical society).

On social media, society becomes a kind of Schrödinger's Cat – known only when we open the app but expected to be there when we are not, functioning on the anxiety of the continuous check, the apprehensive glance; scrolling, posting and liking our way out of a black hole of FOMO – a hole which is crucial to the way social media works.

And yet, unlike the cat in the box; the cat we believe is there whether it's open or closed: social media is an empty box which, for some reason, we believe is full.

The decline of public space and in person relationships have combined with "online space" as both a place of no consequence and a place more important than real life.

The danger is obvious: we view the internet as a more important "place" for our lives than our physical surroundings but, because we can live without accountability online, we can act in ways we wouldn't in our physical lives. We build a life of no consequence.

For example, most people watch porn, [106] many people are addicted, [107] yet their online presence is anonymous, allowing them to consume without accountability to themselves or others. Just as it's harder to buy pornographic magazines, visit a strip club or pay for sex; pornography allows people to indulge in the taboo of sex while evading its consequences, not least its impact on others. Crucially, the viewer avoids accountability to themselves because, as a society, we've been told porn is acceptable and, therefore, the viewer does nothing wrong and its consumption is – despite most evidence to the contrary – harmless. And yet, to be anonymous while engaging in these activities betrays the lie that we're comfortable with its consumption. If we were comfortable, why be anonymous?

And so the allure of porn is that we can engage in something we're told is "normal", yet still reap the excitement of an illicit/explicit encounter. We face the same problems with online gambling or "trolling" on social media. It's easier to be reckless and anonymous at the touch of a button, versus abusing someone in the street, entering a betting shop and so on. We can hide behind legality. We can hide behind normalcy and anonymity. And we can rest in the knowledge that "everyone else does it."

Strength in numbers – supported by a legal framework which refuses to sufficiently regulate the "online space" – is used to justify our own actions in the ethereal realm of the Online, as well as the physical place in which we live. The problem is the internet presents us with infinite opportunities to *not* be ourselves and, through the unleashed Id of the turbulent self, act and consume in a meaningless, anonymous and directionless stupor.

We're always looking for new ways to "be ourselves," to reinvent, to "live our best lives." And, through society-on-demand, we believe the Online is the only place to achieve this: to live a fulfilling life, to be ourselves and succeed.

And let's be honest: it's not surprising.

Society is Dead... Long Live Society

Society sucks.

A world of bingo halls, Wetherspoons and supermarket cafes.

These are – we're told – working class institutions: cornerstones of society.

As such, the very criticism of these icons makes the critic a snob; an avocado-eating, latte-sipping, champagne socialist.

The "Great British High Street," with its cigarette stubs, betting shops and urinated phone booths becomes an untouchable god; a fast food idol in a church of Primarks. This the society we're forced to endure.

So what's the solution?

We have to recognise the problem: that we have no interest in fixing it. Instead, we've replaced our physical society with society-on-demand. It's convenient, it's instant; it's all the time.

And yet, as should be clear by now: this isn't good enough.

We have to address the society in which we live, no matter how difficult, painful or useless it seems.

And, in order to do that, we have to say that some things are better than others; that some things are worth fighting for: and that some things are worth fighting against without the fear of being labelled an enemy of the working class. Some elements of society are damaging and should change, no matter how "elitist" it may sound or how treasured they may be. This will sound controversial. But the longer these problems continue, the more we feel the effects of the Online, the more we recognise the damage it's done and continues to do, the less controversial this will become.

Our history is one of a repeated failure to diagnose our problems. And, if we do, we're often too late to do anything about them.

Climate change is the obvious place to begin, but perhaps some other, more visceral examples, would be useful...

In the UK, the last woman to burn at the stake died less than 250 years ago.[108] Public flogging and the Stocks continued into the 19th century. [109] Public execution, outlawed less than a century ago, was the equivalent of going to the football.

According to the Death Penalty Project:

> *At the beginning of the 18th century, hangings were attended by all classes of society and were considered an excellent day out. The rich would pay handsomely for the best seats to get a good view of the event. By the end of the period, it was mostly the lower classes who were attending executions.[110]*

It wasn't until 1908 that kids under 16 were spared execution, and it wasn't until 1957 that execution was effectively outlawed.[111]

Society has changed and yet, in our progress, we've forgotten how similar we are to our torture-loving, death-jeering, tomato-throwing ascendants.

We look at countries with despotic regimes, brutal punishments and death penalties and, rightly, see them as barbaric: yet we forget just how recent our own history is.

We are – and always have been – a society in constant need of distraction (preferably to the detriment of others).

Our physical society is one of gradual evolution, yet it remains in constant need of correction.

The most deprived communities in the UK account for 18% of betting shops, 29% of Adult Gaming Centres, 30% of Bingo halls and 34% of Family Entertainment Centres ("amusement arcades").[112] According to YouGov, just 15% of people would choose bookmakers for their "ideal" high street. [113] And yet, their very presence is confirmation of their demand. In a country where 42% of over 16s gamble on a monthly basis, we have serious issues.[114]

A high street of bookies and pubs is a statement of values. These values are not just problematic in themselves: they are, equally, a statement about what's *not* valued.

In 2018, gambling contributed almost £9 billion to the economy, an increase of almost 60% since 2010,[115] while library visits were down 28% on the previous decade.[116]

By April 2020, there were more than 10,000 gambling premises [117] looming over a paltry 3,667 libraries. [118] How can a library maintain its appeal while outnumbered almost three to one by gambling sites? Literacy crisis?

No kidding.

Like Coke and the Olympics, McDonalds and the World Cup, TikTok and the Euros: antithetical relationships – whether they're sponsors or competitors – create an equality of meaning; a set of contradictory values for simultaneous use.

Fast food can be paired to physical fitness and the anxiety, consumption and passivity of social media, with elite sport. Our values become weak and duplicitous; a society where porn and fidelity, somehow, go together.[119]

We pledge our allegiance to the status quo because the status quo is sacred. Reluctant to speak, we seek our escape at the altar of indifference.

Acquiescence to inaction is easy – and common. We've accepted a culture that says it's better to escape than challenge, that it's better to despair than hope, that it's better to look out for ourselves than our neighbour. An apathetic culture of cynicism, self-interest and narrow horizons. A Hobbit mentality in a Shireful of Wetherspoons.

How?

Needless to say, it's intentional.

Employers keep their employees rich enough to live but poor enough to require their own exploitation, sapping our desire for an alternative against a backdrop of apathy.

The situation's become so dire that challenging the status quo is not just frowned upon; it's logistically impossible: we wouldn't even know where to begin.

We've elevated society-on-demand to a position of absolute relevance and rely on the Online to find our solutions. We're incapable of envisioning change without the internet as a major player because we've convinced ourselves that technology is always good and ease is the same thing as efficiency and efficacy.

If we are to change this, we need to recognise a few things.

First, the Right has succeeded in shifting politics to the Online; not just as part of a discussion, but as its default location. Physical, societal change – *actual* change – has been replaced by the pacifier of social media.

Working class communities continue to crumble because the efforts of the Left are ploughed into social platforms and online "communities" rather than the physical ones which need their help. Just as political organisation, connections and discussion are controlled by algorithms, heavily monitored and limited on Twitter, Facebook and others; the Left continues to believe it's a good use of its time.

There's no doubt the sharing of information – news stories which don't make it into the mainstream media, for example – benefits from having a free and accessible place to distribute. But, as we've seen – on balance – these platforms are a disaster for progress and the death knell for human relationships, favouring instead tentative "connections" and magnifying the voice of the Right.

If Greta Thunberg and the climate protests took place primarily via hashtag, who knows where we'd be?

And yet, the information required for these protests to succeed *did* come from the likes of Twitter, as did the image of George Floyd's death, filmed by Darnella Frazier (awarded a Pulitzer for recording his murder and uploading it to Facebook), leading to the imprisonment of his killer.[120]

Social media is a tool for information and journalism; not a replacement for conversation, discussion or targeted physical protest (the only source of change that's ever been successful; whether it's the Suffragettes throwing themselves under horses, trade unions on strike, nationwide boycotts or the sit-ins and marches of the civil rights movement): these protests were achieved offline in physical space. Their success – just like the protests of UK Uncut, Extinction Rebellion, Just Stop Oil and Black Lives Matter – was achieved through persistent, targeted, physical acts of resistance.

The very fact that we now have two places to campaign: one in physical society and one online – is itself a major divider in how we spend our time and how successful we are. The major protest movements of the past century were successful because they *had* to take place in person. If social media had been around for the past 100 years, how would this have impacted their efficacy? How would the smartphone and the continual bombardment of entertainment and hashtag activism have impacted the civil rights movement?

This is the importance of a strike. Not that it's an effective means of protest (which it is), but that it's a reminder of physical protest; not just for those on strike who are able to affect change: but as a reminder to everyone else about what actual change looks like, what physical action is, what it can achieve, and – critically – a reminder that people are still doing it.

The changes delivered by strikes are, primarily, changes to workers' professional and personal lives. And yet, strikes also impact the lives of colleagues and the wider organisation. Consequently, they affect the customers and recipients of the organisation's products and services, meaning the public and, by extension, society itself, is affected. This is crucial.

If Tube workers decided to stage a "Twitterstorm" instead of going on strike, what would they achieve? Unions are one of the only surviving examples of a time where change was plotted, organised and achieved through physical action. In that sense, unions are the last bastion of hope against a tidal wave of internet-induced impotence. Strikes are a critical reminder – an example – that physical action doesn't just work: but that it remains *possible*.

Second, we need to accept that while leisure was the preserve of the Elite for thousands of years, "leisure" is now accessible to most of us (even if limited).

It's not enough to settle for the lowest common denominator (to accept "Netflix and chill," gambling, binge-drinking, pornography and sports as a normal part of our lives). We've learned to value unimportant things; pillars of easy conversation and common ground to coalesce around through the asinine chat of the workplace.

These pillars are empowered by the ruling class to trap us in frivolous, damaging activities; designed to keep us spiritually poor yet, at the same time, provide the elusive hope of a better life through winning a bet, a football match or a new TV show.

The go-to forms of leisure and entertainment in our society are a direct result of the intentional, spiritual poverty enforced by the ruling class; be they profit obsessed corporate execs or corrupt politicians looking for complacent electors.

If we are to change this, we need to get to the bottom of each of our remaining obstacles... and that starts with football.

FOOTBALL

Some people believe football is a matter of life and death, I am very disappointed with that attitude. I can assure you it is much, much more important than that.

Bill Shankly.[121]

It's often said, "Football brings people together."

In many ways, that's true.

For 90 minutes, we're physically together. We even have the ability to influence what happens on the pitch ("the 12th man").

And yet, despite unity for ourselves and our teams, each set of fans is united against the other. There's no community or cohesion: there's only opposition; a collection of mutual loathers cramming the anger and frustration of the preceding week into a space of 90 minutes.

So what's the appeal?

Unlike other escapes, sports are oppositional. To support a particular team comes at the expense of not supporting others. In other words: almost everyone has an interest against you and, likewise, you have an interest against almost everyone else.

Fans want their team to win, and that means they're invested in the outcome; emotionally, physically and financially.

This level of commitment means watching games, staying up to date with the latest developments, following the transfer market, debating tactics, fawning over this player, cursing that player, goading fans and screaming at the referee.

Of course, fairness and justice are the presumptive victors. Games should be won by the best teams and the best players. The fan believes football should be fair, that it should be skill, tactics and ability which determine the outcome; it shouldn't be based on the ability to afford players, bad refereeing or fixture schedules.

For the fan, matches are a place of justice away from the society they know: a society which falls infinitely short of the justice and fairness it claims to uphold.

The problem with this is simple: injustice still occurs. The escape is unreliable. Referees make incorrect decisions, players cheat and fairness is difficult to perceive when the manager implements tactical blunders or subs the wrong player, just as a player might naturally underperform.

And this allows us to make rash decisions, to react emotionally in a hyper-charged span of 90 minutes. An injustice against one team necessitates an injustice against the other. In the interest of fairness, if an injustice occurs, it needs to occur on both sides.

For the fan, the most important thing is no longer the sport (the justice on the pitch or the "beauty" of the game): the most important thing is that "our team wins." When our team is the "good guy" and the opposition is the "bad guy," justice is relative. Like the woman accused of witchcraft, burning at the stake is the appropriate punishment; not because it's just, but because they're the "enemy," so who cares?

In football, the desire for justice is short-lived because, inevitably, injustice occurs within the first few minutes of the first game of the season. And, when injustice is guaranteed, the only thing that matters is winning, no matter how it's achieved.

If our team wins then, somehow, we too have won. Our life now has meaning in a meaningless society and – as a reward for the stress we've endured – we claim an identity in a club that suffers injustice but triumphs all the same. We're heroes.

And yet, in addition to justice, the fan is compelled in other ways; primarily, the idea of a "clean slate," something almost completely impossible in society's current state.

With each season comes new hope. As the season progresses, this hope either increases or decreases, depending on how well our team plays.

The idea of a clean slate is, like justice, an idea we're often denied in the rest of our lives.

If we make a mistake or something bad happens, we can't simply look to next year for everything to start again from a neutral position, as if the last year didn't happen (much as our society tries to convince us that the "New Year" is, somehow, a decisive break with the previous one).

Of course, these delusions are obvious: but they're rarely considered. Instead, like other parts of society-on-demand, the delusions of damaging interests and collusions of an economy based on retreat are accepted as normal, even good; used as a basis for general socialisation (the lowest common denominator) and the tenuous logistics of navigating the workplace and, with it, wider society.

In this context, football provides the hope necessary to escape the despair of reality. And yet, to invest our hopes and dreams on a trivial outcome – a football match – we let our lives regress into irrelevance, still burdened by unresolved problems, having done nothing to alleviate them; choosing instead to surrender our own agency and forego the actions of our own power, giving our entire mental and emotional state to a football club. The more we invest in football the more we starve ourselves of meaningful hope and progress; and the less possible change becomes.

Our concerns become not the welfare of others who, in the context of capitalism, are the opposition. Instead, our concerns become, "How is my team going to do this week?" and, "How can I make more money to live the lifestyle I want?"

Sport is a servant of capitalism. It trains us to oppose not the government, but each other: and for arbitrary reasons. To see everyone as a threat to our own desires; teaching us to define our selves by defeating others, not helping them. And this is made possible through the fan, whose obsession displaces everything else; whose mindset is, fundamentally, oppositional. The fan has nothing better to do than watch sport and use their own lives in the pursuit of someone else's glory: with no ability to affect the outcome.

Families are forced apart because they spend more time thinking about football than meaningful time with their families. Between work, school and sleep, vacant mental space is important, yet it's occupied by football. Entire weeks are ruined based on the result of a weekend's match. When we base our lives on a weekly game whose result is – for most of us – completely out of our control (shouting at the TV does nothing): we find ourselves living for the next event, defining our lives by the hope of the next game, not genuine hope for our own lives.

We stay in jobs we don't like and suffer the misery of our lives because the next game is only six days away: our regular dose of meaning. And what is our meaning? Opposition.

As an ex-fan, I'd watch games and wish "my" players would literally break the legs of players from the opposing team; such is the absurd animosity for kicking a ball. Should an opposition player dive into a dirty, potentially career ending tackle, then the law of natural justice says they, too, should have a career ending injury. We believe this so strongly that, even as I write this, I feel my blood boiling (and I stopped watching football two years ago).

We build these theatres – these colosseums – where we let our emotions loose; where we can indulge our base instincts, entering orgies of uncontrolled passion, imbibing the cup of animalistic power.

What's more, when we do this, we believe we're fine – that we're safe – confined to a specific time and place, a particular event of frustration.

And yet, just as pornography has long-term effects (as we'll see), and just as social media has a lasting impact on the way we think, feel and communicate: our feelings are not confined to a specific time and place. We cannot imbibe, flick a switch and go back to normal. We cannot leave a highly emotional scene and walk away level-headed as a fully-functioning, healthy human being. We are, fortuitously, all too human for that.

Which means we carry these animalised minds and behaviours – these nihilistic emotions – with us throughout our lives, with enough regular doses of meaning through the weekly match to maintain a base level of frustration, anger and injustice; often masked by the delusional hope that if our team wins at the weekend, we'll have a chance of winning something completely pointless.

One game doesn't make us obsessive. Just as a cigarette doesn't make someone addicted (unless we're predisposed for that particular form of abuse).

But, with repetition and practice; with the absence of meaning and satisfaction in other significant areas of our lives then, of course, we can expect to fill that absence with damaging alternatives.

Society – at the encouragement of government – is all too happy to indulge us; seeking new ways to improve the efficiency of locking us into prisons of impotence.

Like all aspects of society-on-demand, we are engaged in a continuous battle for our will; to actively fight against the forces of pervasive digital entertainment, as the main tool of capitalist control. Again, this doesn't mean a rejection of digital entertainment. It means a rejection of continuous engagement, away from the oppression of society-on-demand, to consume consciously and occasionally, rather than absent-mindedly, leading to the prioritisation of passive entertainment and consumption as our default use of free time.

What Changed?

Of course, sport in itself is not an opium of the people. Sport was attended regularly throughout the 20th century; yet we still had mass protests, effective trade unions and class awareness; leading to solidarity and political change.

The problems began when sport became divorced from its once-a-week attendance (for example, the weekend football fixture) and became, instead, a twenty-four-seven, digitally dominant narrative.

Rather than the weekly match remaining a point of community cohesion and solidarity – a social event – a scheduled break in the everyday life of working class community: football became an industry based on continuous updates and individual followings; watchable on TV and, today, online, with its endless highlights, transfer rumours, interviews, photos, videos and analysis – plus the biggest distraction of all: *user-generated content and the desire for relevance.*

There are now thousands of club fan sites, podcasts, YouTube channels and social media accounts, in addition to club-generated content.

The mainstream media continues its role to provide match reports, interviews and analysis; yet its own fingers have extended well beyond print and entered into its own internet empire.

The only reason clubs are able to make so much money is because of fan engagement and consumption, and the only way clubs have as many fans as they do (in many cases, tens of millions and, in some cases, even hundreds of millions), is by amassing individual, disparate and "disconnected" fans through society-on-demand.

This is the problem. Not that sports clubs exist, nor the working class traditions accompanying them. But that sport itself has been removed from the working class roots it purports to uphold. Clubs have been removed from a network of working class communities – not by choice – but because these roots were removed hook, line and sinker by successive governments, to the benefit of the ruling class and its corporate allies.

When the trivialities of sport consume us, something else is ignored or suppressed. Some of you may disagree. And yet, if sport isn't a triviality, what is it? If sport is not ultimately meaningless, if sport does nothing to advance the causes of society and is not a place (for the vast majority of fans) – of physical and personal solidarity – then it is meaningless. And that's OK. Because it's supposed to be. *Sport is supposed to be sport.* It's supposed to be fun and challenging as good social, mental and physical exercise.

But when we elevate football to the place of a god – something which has complete power over our own lives – then we are allowing idols to get in the way of what really matters.

When our entire week, every week, is based on the result of a football match, then we fail. Even if our team wins, we've failed by transferring our own meaning and value, our own success, onto a football club – something completely out of our control – instead of finding meaning in our own lives and the lives of others.

As soon as we recognise that it is not our opposition to other clubs that defines us, but football's opposition to *us,* then we can begin to correct this course and find meaning in our own lives, and those of others, again.

And for that, we're going to need something game changing...

Solutions

As we've seen, football is, by nature, oppositional.

The more a team wins, the greater their chance of winning a trophy and, the more they lose, the greater their chance of relegation or, worse, falling short of expectations.

While musicians, actors and artists perform for the joy of playing; the footballer plays to compete. And while the creativity of the players is essential to entertainment, the purpose of sport is not self-expression or creative transcendence: it's competition.

When a painter sits at an easal or a musician at the drums, their instinct isn't to outperform someone else: it's to express themselves. If that means others can derive joy, inspiration or meaning from their contribution, even better.

And yet, if the purpose of their instruments was to compete with other artists, we'd destroy self-expression in the pursuit of victory. A defender won't risk a rabona in their own box. Self-expression is sacrificed for the purpose of the game: to beat the other team.

The Goliath that football's become since the introduction of the Premier League has created a culture of reliance, passivity and idolatry; placing football above all else and allowing it to dominate our lives.

In order to change this and regain our lives, we need to reduce the importance of opposition.

Reducing the importance of opposition would mean reducing the level of care, anxiety, stress and dominance of football. Without the significance of winning and losing, we can reduce football's control over our lives and the associated damage it causes. This would also have a huge impact on how we view society generally, removing the arbitrary barrier of which clubs we support.

How do we achieve this?

By reducing the importance of failure.

The Super League

In April 2021, plans were announced to launch a "European Super League."

The Super League would see the biggest clubs in Europe launch a new football franchise, a franchise from which clubs can't be relegated, playing games throughout the year that lacked substantial consequence. Everyone's a winner.

In this country, there are lots of things you can do. You can binge drink, you can gamble (and sport positively encourages both), you can watch porn, you can buy clothes made in sweat shops and eggs from caged hens. You can promote racism and publish hate. You can buy factory-farmed meat from animals tortured to death. You can charge extortionate rents and let uninhabitable housing. You can even host parties during lockdown (if you're the Prime Minister): *but you cannot trivialise football.*

And that, essentially, is what the Super League did. In a game which no longer holds any negative consequences for the clubs involved; when the threat of relegation is removed: games become trivial.

As ex-footballer and Sky Football pundit, Gary Neville observed:

> *I spent 25 years under a manager here playing when every single team talk he talked about the ability to do the right thing, work hard, to do the right things every single match, to fight to the end - never feel entitled, never feel complacent, come back every year and do it again. Not 'we can have a year off because we're in a franchise league and we don't go down'. That is not what football in this country is about.*[122]

And yet, the ESL was not a replacement for England's main competition, the Premier League. Nor was it a replacement for other cup competitions. It was, instead, in addition to these things (although, logistically, it was probably a replacement for clubs' involvement in the Champions League).

Regardless, the football community was united in its opposition, with pundits, governing bodies and the vast majority of fans opposed, with almost 70% of fans "strongly opposed."[123]

Protests took place on social media and outside stadiums, with negative coverage provided on mainstream news channels and, of course, the wider press, who rely on football as a major source of reporting.

Significantly, the UK government also intervened, with the Culture Secretary stating: "We will put everything on the table to prevent this from happening. We are examining every option from governance reform to competition law, and mechanisms that allow football to take place."[124]

Even Prince William, as head of the FA, claimed, "Now, more than ever, we must protect the entire football community – from the top level to the grassroots – and the values of competition and fairness at its core."[125]

Within a few days, the ESL was scrapped.

Something as insignificant as a game – of kicking a ball – succeeded in uniting one of the most right-wing, reactionary, elitist governments in the UK's history, with millions of poor, low and middle-income fans across the country.

The average fan of the six Premier League clubs enrolled in the Super League earned £566.46 a week. The average player for these clubs earned £109,818.83 per week; almost 200 times the income of the average supporter.[126]

Government intervention in the ESL was not only popular: it was, from the perspective of the ruling class, necessary. The cost of non-intervention could have been catastrophic for the "football pyramid" (the process by which teams gain promotion or relegation through what should be a tough but fair process) and, with it, the destabilisation of the main source of entertainment and purpose in the country.[127]

Without football, millions of people would suddenly have the free time, resources and – critically – emotional energy required to demand societal change; all of which have been compromised for decades through the promise of weekly football games.

The placation of the working class through football has been incredibly effective, beginning more than thirty years ago with the creation of the Premier League.

Establishing what we now call "the modern game," the Premier League was launched in the early 90s, following visceral attacks on working class communities by Thatcher.

The unions were largely crushed and the working class had, for all intents and purposes, lost a decades long battle against privatisation and deregulation, culminating in the Labour Party – the traditional political voice of the working class – shifting decisively to the Right just two years later under Tony Blair. Why does this matter?

The Premier League was the beginning of regular broadcast football. It was the start of mass consumption, mass marketing and advertising.

The correlation between the imposition of a new age of football through the Premier League and handing Rupert Murdoch's BSkyB the exclusive broadcasting rights, isn't a coincidence.

The number of televised games has been growing almost every year, beginning at just 60 games a season in the 90s, before almost doubling in the early 2000s, to 200 games a season in 2021-22.[128]

When television rights are mixed with online content, it's not hard to see how society-on-demand has consumed arguably the most sacred pastime in the country's history, aiding the placation which has since ensued.

The growth of TV revenue and the increasing number of viewers has delivered a growth contribution of 840% since 1999, fuelled by broadcast rights and the 43 million people who watch the Premier League on TV in the UK alone.[129]

There's even been a campaign – led by Sky Bet – to make Transfer Deadline Day a bank holiday, as if we should deify it any further.[130]

Since the Premier League's introduction, there's been no major rebuild of the union movement, privatisation has continued to other industries, labour laws remain weak and consumerism has reached new heights.[131]

Just as smartphones and social media took-off in the wake of the financial crash, football did the same in the wake of political and economic crises. And, given that we have never truly recovered from these crises, football continues to grow, maintaining its relevance in the lives of millions of people.

The deregulation of gambling and the encouragement of alcohol use has further cemented a shift away from social cohesion to society-on-demand through the idolisation of football.[132]

60% of clubs in England's top footballing leagues advertised gambling on their shirts, [133] and England's Championship, League One and League Two divisions are sponsored by Sky Bet.[134] With continuous advertisements to "gamble responsibly" on TVs across the country and with clubs accepting sponsorships from these companies – combined with the proliferation of online gambling – it's no surprise that engagement's high.[135]

And yet, this shows no sign of abating, with the gambling industry claiming one out of every six minutes of ad time during the 2018 World Cup.[136]

In a crowded pub on a derby weekend, it's too easy to reach into your pocket, grab your phone and place a bet. The ubiquity of the smartphone extends to all times and places.

For students, it's even worse, with 80% of students gambling on a weekly basis, and 35% of them using student loans to do so, spending over £30 a week. 41% even skipped lectures and social events to gamble, despite 25% of activity being carried out online.[137] But the problems don't end here.

Sky Bet's *Super 6*, a free gambling competition where players can guess six correct scores for a chance of winning a cash prize, is a gateway drug into the wider betting infrastructure.[138] Other gambling companies do the same, with regular advertising and "free bets."

Many of these companies have phone apps, enabling the user to bet at a moment's notice.

Of course, this level of exposure is not without consequence, making its way into seemingly innocent ventures such as fantasy football; a typically free, online game played by millions of people. Its heavier users report "mild low mood" even when *thinking* about the game, as well as causing mild anxiety and disruption to their lives.[139]

Like other pillars of society-on-demand, companies benefit from compulsive use to the detriment of the user, with huge consequences for mental health, influencing the further proliferation of damaging activities in a carnivorous cycle of cause and effect.

And so, contrary to the government, media, fans, clubs and institutions of the game: the ESL presented an opportunity. An opportunity to weaken the dominance of football, to transform it from "a matter of life and death" into an amusement; something like American baseball: a sport without consequence, culling its ability to dominate our lives.

Like many aspects of society-on-demand, if it were as simple as choosing not to take part, self-regulating our behaviour or taking responsibility for our actions: we'd be fine.

And yet, these problems, in most instances, are getting worse; not because we shirk our responsibilities, but because we face a deliberate and ruthless attack from these industries.

Like the product design of Facebook and TikTok, the normalisation of porn or the ubiquitous use of smartphones; football and the forces it suppresses – of social cohesion and progressive change – relies on the obsequious presence of gambling and alcohol to charge the batteries of overworked, underpaid and frustrated fans, whose sole purpose in life has become the club they support.

We give these idols our energy, passion and allegiance. And while we can, in theory, take control of our own lives, we cannot control a culture which is, clearly, out of control.

But what if, instead of spending our lives worshiping the talents of others, we discovered our own? What if, instead of living for the next game, we lived for today? What if, instead of pouring our frustration and handing our attention to those earning 200 times our own salary, instead of giving our lives to an industry fuelled by gambling, alcohol and social media, we instead devoted our lives to making life better?

The ESL was a chance to begin this.

Instead, the establishment, and those who'd consider themselves anything else, failed to remove a system which controls the schedule of our lives, our emotional state and mental focus; where a life of stability, peace and fulfilment is replaced by a rollercoaster of 90 minutes.

For those claiming the football pyramid is essential – for the Gary Nevilles, football associations, league leaders, managers, fans and others – it is only essential in its current form: of private companies owning clubs, allowing them to take on debt, threatening their existence and driving them into the ground. It is private ownership and the minority control of clubs that threaten the stability of football.

A quick fix would be to set a reasonable wage cap, disallow clubs from taking on debt and putting them in the hands of local supporters.

This would mean no more sponsorships (avoiding the promotion of gambling and alcohol), it would mean no major broadcast deals (removing the spectacle of football and allowing it to be a local, community based sport) and it would mean fans being empowered to make decisions without suffering the iniquities and anxieties of watching corporate leaders make stupid mistakes.

Each club would be financially sustainable, able to suffer relegation or enjoy promotion without financial penalty.

It would, in short, be the first step of returning football to a sport, not a god.

The Result

Every crisis – whether it's the obliteration of the labour movement in the 80s, the financial crash of 2008 or the pandemic of 2020 and the ensuing cost of living crisis, exacerbated by Brexit – has been followed by new and exaggerated modes of escape.

Crises are no longer allowed to be digested and experienced. We're no longer allowed to suffer. Crisis is now an underlying feature of our existence, a normal part of everyday life, by virtue of the fact that, a. there have been so many and, b. they're not addressed.

As soon as we begin to address one crisis, another one follows. Before we know it, we're unable to properly organise and generate a sufficient response; unable to compose a compelling narrative or plan for change.

Our society needs radical solutions: and radical escape is not one of them. But it's the only response we seem capable of mustering; the only "solution" we believe in.

The Premier League and modern football, with its funding structures and broadcasting rights, leading to greater consumption and the idolatry of sport; the financial crash and the rise of internet 2.0 – of fast broadband speeds, social media and smartphones – and Covid-19 ensuring the further digitisation of culture; have firmly established society-on-demand as our default mode of escape, laying the groundwork for future developments such as the "metaverse," the increasing need for smartphones to access basic services, the widening of delivery networks and logistics for online shopping, the closure of cinemas and failure of other cultural institutions, further reducing public space and moving society online.

With the exception of Black Lives Matter in the middle of global lockdowns, the efficacy of resistance over the past thirty years, with only a handful of major strikes (with varying results) and almost no effective protests (the Iraq War protest failed, the anti-Brexit protests failed, the tuition fees protests failed, and so on); we have accepted a narrative that protest is futile and the system is beyond change; further endangering protest as a viable means of organisation; relegating resistance to a football match.

And yet, the wider cultural movement behind climate activism over the last decade has been effective. What began as protest succeeded in transforming itself into a movement, embedding itself in wider political discourse and social engagement. As with Black Lives Matter, consistency of protest and clarity of purpose were essential.

These protests gave rise to further acts of resistance such as the forcible removal of slave trader, Edward Coulston's statue and acts of civil disobedience via Extinction Rebellion and Just Stop Oil who, incidentally, targeted Premier League football games as an effective method of protest, tying themselves to goalposts and wearing t-shirts stating, "Just Stop Oil", with a link to their website for more information.[140] A clear message, with a simple call to action, at the biggest events in the country.

But it wasn't until Labour elected Jeremy Corbyn in 2015 that disparate issues were presented as a holistic set of proposals; a philosophy of the problems we face and how they're linked to an unjust economic system, allowing the party to make significant gains in the 2017 election. Despite winning the argument on austerity, this philosophy was quickly forgotten under the leadership of Keir Starmer, opting instead for messaging around "values" rather than policies of fundamental change through a coherent political narrative.

And yet, while the issues of racism and climate change have breached public consciousness, allowing the public to understand their importance: public consciousness isn't enough. Society-on-demand remains effective even when these movements are popularised through football, validated by the establishment. When Black Lives Matter is combined with the spectacle of football, the issue is construed as entertainment, damaging its political relevance and personalising its problems, ignoring systemic injustice.

Players taking the knee is important: and yet, the campaigns of "Kick It Out" (active for years in Premier League football) and support for BLM, have failed; unable to reduce systemic racism, nor destroy its enablers.

In 2020, the Premier League announced its support for players taking the knee or displaying "Black Lives Matter" on their shirts, endorsed by players from each club:

> *We, the Players, stand together with the singular objective of eradicating racial prejudice wherever it exists, to bring about a global society of inclusion, respect, and equal opportunities for All,*

regardless of their colour or creed. This symbol is a sign of unity from all Players, all Staff, all Clubs, all Match Officials and the Premier League #blacklivesmatter #playerstogether.[141]

Unlike Just Stop Oil, who actively disrupted games through unsanctioned acts of resistance, the Premier League and its players opted instead for sanctioned, convenient and, consequently, ineffective displays of support, choosing to focus on prejudice instead of systemic injustice.

When "protest" takes place with the agreement of those we're protesting against, it's not protest: it's acquiescence. And, in the case of anti-racism in football, protest was actively encouraged, demonstrating just how ineffective these protests would be.

When the status quo continues to fail, civil resistance is the only option; to act against the wishes of the status quo. And yet, despite decades of racist abuse and systemic injustice, the most we're willing to risk is knee cramp.

Instead, taking the knee should be followed by strike action, precisely against the wishes of football's governing bodies; a refusal to play until radical reforms are introduced and legislation secured.

The government's success – of embedding impotence through escape versus societal change, *even when public consciousness is breached and the awareness of injustice secured* – is obvious. Climate change continues at pace. Racism remains systemic, with no sign of improvement.

Two years on, players are still taking the knee and, two years on, the officers who strip searched Child Q – a black fifteen year old, on school premises, even going so far as to remove her sanitary pad – are put on "desk duty" for their "regrettable" actions. [142] Destroying a child's life through a humiliating strip search is regrettable, the punishment for which isn't the sack, or even a suspension: it's desk duty, pending investigation.

In the last three years alone, the Met Police conducted more than 5,000 strip searches on children, some of whom were as young as 10. 75% were from ethnically diverse backgrounds, and this only included children who were arrested first; which means Child Q – and those like her – wouldn't have been counted. [143]

Once again, we find the apathy generated by society-on-demand influencing not just the prevention of protest: but actively diluting it on the rare occasion it occurs.

How is this possible?

Because football is more important than justice.

The hypocrisy of society-on-demand (as we saw with the creators of social media apps, limiting access for their own kids while destroying the lives of others) allows us to display solidarity through lip service – online or in person – before forgetting all about it.

And yet, the establishment doesn't rest. Despite the influence of society-on-demand even to physical space, the government would be careless to not back its success with legislation, which is why the *Police, Crime, Sentencing and Courts Bill* attempts to "stop disruptive protests from disproportionately infringing on the rights and freedoms of others",[144] fundamentally changing the nature of protest; making it increasingly difficult to protest in person, even as individuals.

The bill would also, in a further attack on public space, "strengthen police powers to tackle unauthorised encampments",[145] threatening the livelihoods of Traveller communities across the country, making this lifestyle increasingly difficult for anyone seeking a life away from the unaffordable costs of rent, mortgages and other forms of economic oppression; a culture of rising popularity exemplified in Chloé Zhao's *Nomadland*, finding its appeal in a post-Covid world.[146]

And while the government doubles-down on its victories, the Left is incapable of acting to achieve even basic change.

The challenge we face is clear: is a cultural movement based on a wider critique of capitalism with consistent, physical protest going to win against the systemic, deeply entrenched apathy delivered and empowered by society-on-demand?

The days of protesting once and hoping for the best are over. What's required now is a cultural movement, accompanied by physical action through persistent, physical campaigns and protest, in person discussions and physical relationships. Physical structures and networks of people must be the basis of any political movement to avoid the disruption of society-on-demand with its algorithms, lack of nuance and encouragement to "perform" through hyperbolic posts and divisive content, not to mention the unavoidable crossover of entertainment through the smartphone.

We need to resist the clear battle lines between "sides", exemplified in sport and championed on social media. We need to discuss and convince in nuanced, human conversation, not rely on the division these platforms impose. This division places us on a never-ending quest for the perfect ally: an ally which doesn't exist. Just as the Online encourages us to create a perfect Self, it also imposes this desire for perfection onto others, encouraging us to focus on our differences and, worse, to devalue each other *for* these differences, instead of recognising the strength of our diversity; of each person, personality and skillset.

-

Football has conditioned us to win; to oppose; to hope. And yet, instead of directing these lessons at the government, we've confined them to society-on-demand; to an industry which champions the surrender of agency, the corruption of values, the glory of apathy. Instead of exerting our own effort, we allow others to do it for us, outsourcing our struggle to the football pitch, where the super-rich carry our hopes for a trophy we'll never lift in a game we didn't play. And, when our avatars of hope, meaning and success are threatened with irrelevance, we rise to their defence; kneeling before the status quo, begging the elite to save the Escape.

So long as this continues – so long as the victory of a football club is placed above the victory of political change: we will continue to fail; seduced by the escape of society-on-demand.

In the words of Fred Hampton, "If you dare to struggle, then you dare to win. If you dare not to struggle, you don't deserve to win."[147]

It's entirely up to us.

At this point, it's worth taking stock.

So far, we've seen the effects of smartphones; platforming our obstacles and enabling society-on-demand as an ever present threat; we've seen the impact of social media on our mental health and how it fundamentally changes the nature of our identity, how we communicate and relate to each other, as well as its influence over politics, causing impotence and division; and we've seen how football placates us with spectacle and the idol of false hope, reducing us to trivial interests; sapping our time and energy through continuous digital content.

But there is another obstacle – a fundamental piece of the puzzle – that we've not fully addressed.

Unlike the other issues we've faced, pornography is unique, occupying a publicly rejected yet culturally accepted space.

Like other issues we've addressed, porn is just as ubiquitous, just as present and just as damaging to our mental health and relationships; reducing others to "content" and, worse still, objects.

And yet, pornography goes largely unchallenged, benefiting from its position as both a publicly illicit yet privately implicit activity; a cultural staple we're expected to indulge, but in private.

Despite this, porn is everywhere: on the train, on the bus; even in school. And while public consumption is likely to make most people extremely uncomfortable, there are no laws against it.

Professor Clare McGlynn of Durham University, a legal specialist, likened the public consumption of pornography to "reading a book." The user is "viewing lawful material which is freely available, and restricting people's access to it presents other challenges."[148]

BBC Journalist Siobhann Tighe wrote about her experience sitting next to a passenger on the bus who began watching porn on their phone.[149] This experience is not uncommon. A subsequent article in *BBC Magazine* found that many people are exposed to porn in public, against their wishes.

Train guards, for example, are encountering this on a regular basis, describing it as "an increasing problem."[150]

Others recall children watching porn in McDonalds, sound blaring, to the complaints of other customers. Others watch it on long distance flights, at airports or even in restaurants.[151]

According to one former primary school teacher, now an expert on child sexual abuse:

> *Children don't have to be able to type to see porn – it can be sent to them or shown to them on someone else's phone. They see it at school, in the corridors, in the bathrooms, on the bus. There is just no censor on any of it – one video leads to another. If you can imagine it, it exists as porn, and children are seeing it.*[152]

Once again, we find ourselves unable to escape the presence of society-on-demand, imposing itself without our consent.

In the past, we'd have to physically go into a magazine to view content, whether it was advertising, gossip, porn, whatever. Once the magazine was closed, so were our minds. Porn was something we did: now it's something we are.

Locking our phones, closing the browser or changing the channel isn't enough. The possibility of more porn – a never ending chasm of content – plagues our minds, challenging us to exhaust a near endless supply of material.

A magazine, on the other hand, is a fixed thing with a set number of pictures. The content remains the same. If you want more pictures, you buy another magazine. And even these are limited.

But it's not just the internet.

Today, a quick search in the *QuoDB* movie database returns over 7,000 references to "porn" across a handful of movies and TV shows,[153] including family comedy series, *Zoe 101*. (This show was later nominated for "Outstanding Children's Programme" at the Emmys).[154]

Porn is the unspoken pandemic, made worse through the use of personal devices, ease of access and the proliferation of content.

Unsurprisingly, the main culprit is that "revolutionary" device: the smartphone.

Pornhub, the UK's most visited porn site, was primarily accessed via smartphone in 2020 (77%),[155] and this has no doubt increased since then, in line with other trends (in 2021, 83% of global users accessed the site via smartphone).[156]

That most porn is viewed free of charge is increasingly problematic when combined with immediate access, yet even paid services like Pornhub Premium are used by 7% of the adult population, alongside XHamster Premium – another popular porn site – used by almost 10%.

And yet, its use is unevenly distributed among age groups, with Gen Z and Millennials making up 42% of all porn users[157] and almost one in three men aged 18 to 25 feeling addicted.[158]

75% of men and 33% of women aged 18 to 24 visited Pornhub in September 2020 alone, with the average minutes per visitor for the five most visited sites at just over fifty minutes.[159]

And yet, these statistics capture only a fraction of pornographic material. It doesn't include the plethora of explicit TV shows, movies and magazines, nor pornography on social media, smaller websites, etc.

Growing up in the mid-2000s, porn was a normal part of adolescence. Occasionally accessed, somewhat enjoyed but, crucially, quickly forgotten. For young people today, it's impossible to avoid and, increasingly, to forget.

Almost half of 11 to 16 year olds have seen porn online,[160] more than half of 11 to 13 year olds have been exposed to pornographic content, yet 60% of them were exposed unintentionally.[161] If that wasn't bad enough, 10% of 12 to 13 year olds now fear they're addicted.[162]

This is translating itself in the real world, with 12% of 12 to 13 year olds having created or taken part in sexually explicit videos. [163] The more normalised pornography becomes, the more easily sex is weaponised and used among younger age groups.

Secondary schools have become hubs of abuse, where pornographic culture has become normalised, with kids as young as 14 performing sex acts and where sexually explicit images have become a form of validation.[164] And yet the influence of porn is most notable in the perception of body image. In the words of one secondary school teacher:

> *I was on break time duty and I heard a boy say 'I put my hand in her pants and it was like a forest and I was quick out of there.' It's the accepted norm amongst the girls that you shave it all off - a totally unspoken rule",* and, when it to comes to sex education, if *"teachers don't feel confident talking about these things"* then *"it's clear we're setting them up to go on to a porn website to learn about sex."*[165]

The teacher goes on to say that social media, pornography and ease of access have created "an infected generation that no longer sees the gravitas of sex." [166] Unfortunately, it doesn't end here.

Over the last few years, Hentai – a type of cartoon porn based on Japanese anime – has become the default pornography of choice for Gen Z, with 76% more likely to watch it than older age groups. In 2021 it was the most popular search term on Pornhub,[167] up from second place in 2019[168] and second only to "Japanese," which dropped to second place in 2021. (Incidentally, the passenger sitting next to Journalist Siobhann Tighe was also watching animated porn).[169]

The popularity of these searches is a disturbing – yet consistent – insight into the mental shifts we're seeing in wider society.

The use of cartoons as the pornography of choice (with Gen X significantly more likely to watch pornographic cartoons than other age groups) betrays an increasing lack of interest in – even repulsion of – real human beings.

In the words of one viewer, "a real female of course smells, is dirty... of course because it's a human being, it has lots of things... so we have this anime. Isn't it clean and pretty?"[170]

Even if we treat this consumer as a minority (and there's little evidence to do so), something as innocuous as a lack of interest becomes a double-edged sword: a lack of interest means the abuse of people is restricted and the perception of women as sex objects is less easily established; and yet this lack of interest also achieves a further distancing of ourselves from others; the prioritisation of cartoons over the physical society in which we live and the real human beings within it. Once again, we're witnessing the continued decline of physicality; an increasingly irrelevant feature of our existence.

After all, we'd be hard pressed to conclude that animated porn has been popularised through a moral aversion against the use of real human beings, as if sexual exploitation has driven a rejection of traditional porn in a kind of perverse, pornographic boycott.

If we were feeling generous, we might say that – through animation – porn remains decisively in the fantasy realm, where a crossover to real life is seen as impossible, with porn *itself* acknowledged as a perverse, delusional fantasy.

On the face of it, this is a good thing. Re-emphasising fantasy as fiction can render the crossover to reality more difficult, limiting its applicability from fantasy to reality.

And yet, the damage to the viewer – of indulging in explicit, image-driven fantasy – remains, regardless of whether the object of our lust is real.

The justification of, "I'm not bad, I'm just drawn that way",[171] is a kind of Rabbit-out-of-a-hat excuse to justify our indulgence. And yet, to distinguish between "real" porn as bad and animation as "fine" is to say personal damage is acceptable, so long as we're not harming anyone else. The truth, of course, is that millions of people engaging in psychologically damaging activity *does* have an impact on others; changing our relationships, social involvement and perception of each other, not least running the risk of addiction and other crises. The reduction of liberty and freedom to personal choice, ignoring its wider social and political impact, is fundamentally damaging to individuals and wider society; whether that's through pornography or other forms of digital entertainment. The damage is done

87

because the user is, themselves, damaged. To see our personal circumstance as separate from wider society is not just anti-human: it's anti-fact.

When a majority of men and a significant minority of women watch porn on a regular basis,[172] we live in a society where millions of people – through pornography alone – are living with a fundamentally corrupt perception of themselves and others: with devastating consequences.

Relationships

Porn destabilises existing relationships; with the probability of divorce doubling for individuals who begin watching porn during marriage. The average 20 year old who doesn't watch porn has a 6% chance of divorce, while those who begin watching porn during marriage have a 51% chance. 28% of 30 year olds who begin watching porn are expected to divorce, along with 12% of 40 year olds, before tailing-off among older age groups.[173]

According to a study of almost 1,800 US adults, not only is pornography linked to the failure of committed relationships, it's also linked to adverse impacts within relationships; on satisfaction, stability and communication, no doubt impacting their stability or, at the very least, happiness.[174]

But it's not just porn which negatively affects our relationships.

Typically viewed as a more wholesome endeavour, online dating is a major source of unhappiness; lowering self-esteem and increasing depression amongst users.[175]

The nature of dating apps – just like social media – encourages compulsive use.

Relying heavily on shorthand and confining conversation to texts and images, restricting relationships to the mobile phone: the same problems that exist on social media will, inevitably, plague apps which rely on similar processes. Combine these processes with a romantic or sexual motivation, and these issues can become entrenched in the relationship before it's even begun.

Communication via emoji – as with social media – finds its voice on dating apps, with the "tears of joy" emoji the most used across the top five dating applications.[176] What level of expectation does this set?

One can easily imagine how, on meeting in person, the jokes don't quite land as they did online, the tension becomes awkward, the eye contact, avoided, and the tears of joy emoji which enabled the date in the first place is quickly replaced by the pensive frown of disappointment, all the while mocked by the upside-down-smiley-face of the companies which brought them there.

A relationship built on swipes and emojis is going to have mixed results at best; with almost 2 out of 5 users feeling more frustrated than hopeful, and almost 1 in 5 feeling more pessimistic than optimistic.[177]

And yet, like most things, experience varies significantly by demographic.

For example, 6 in 10 women aged 18 to 34 received unwanted messages after saying they weren't interested, 57% received sexually explicit content they didn't ask for, 44% were called an offensive name and almost one in five were threatened with physical harm.[178]

This shouldn't be surprising.

When sex-on-demand through pornography is just a click away from dating apps, it doesn't take a genius to figure out that the objectification of women and relationships in a pornographic culture influences behaviour across the board – even through apps purportedly focused on relationships, not hook-ups.

And yet, the myth of online success translating to physical success rears its head again, with most Americans claiming relationships established online are just as successful as those established in person, despite just one in ten achieving a committed relationship that started online.[179]

The disconnect between perception and reality; the belief in the empowerment of the Online; continues to prejudice and blind our lived experience.

For sites like Tinder, the most widely used dating app in the world, this delusion serves nicely.

A study of mostly undergraduate students by the *American Psychological* Association found that:

> *As a result of how the app works and what it requires of its users, people who are on Tinder after a while may begin to feel depersonalised and disposable in their social interactions, develop heightened awareness (and criticism) of their looks and bodies and believe that there is always something better around the corner, or rather with the next swipe of their screen, even while questioning their own worth.[180]*

The study also found that "body dissatisfaction", "comparing oneself physically to others" and "relying on media for information on appearance and attractiveness" were as applicable to men as they were to women.[181]

These apps often use gimmicks to maintain user interest and engagement. For example, the rollout of Tinder's "music mode" in December 2021 enabled users to link their Spotify accounts to their Tinder profiles, allowing them to choose "that one song that defines them inside and out" – a song that plays automatically when a user visits their profile. Needless to say, this is already a hit with Gen Z, 40% of whom enabled this function at the time of rollout.[182]

And isn't this the essence of online dating? That, through a handful of curated images, messages, videos and music, we're empowered to find the "perfect match?"

The truth is, most apps aren't designed for long term relationships. The business model of Tinder doesn't lend itself to commitment because it requires users. If you're in a committed relationship, you won't have a use for it and, consequently, will either delete it or stop using it. Instead, most apps function (as the study above suggests) to encourage users to believe they're never done: that there's always someone better. To quote Tinder directly, "Some sites, like Hinge and eharmony, are designed for long-term relationships, but at Tinder, we're all about the experience, and offer possibilities for whatever you're looking for."[183]

As with any system optimised for compulsive, continuous use: we are engaged in a war against time.

And yet, even if we win – if we lay down our phones and drag ourselves away from the allure of swiping, scrolling and, in this case, gawping – we remain engaged in a war for our selves; a self uncorrupted by algorithms, deforming and reshaping our brains with dopamine death bombs analogous to cocaine; tearing through the hallways of our veins and hammering the doors of our minds.[184] [185]

Smartphones, as we've seen, are the main culprit here, alongside a sexually-charged, pornographically-implicit culture, both online and off.

And yet, not only is the consumption of porn reaching and exploiting younger age groups, but these same demographics are just as likely to compulsively use social media and smartphones, suffering poor mental health generally. In this context, porn becomes the logical self-medication for an internet-based society.

A study of more than 8,000 adults in the *International Journal of Environmental Research and Public Health*, found those suffering mental health problems "may be drawn to interactive, digital forms of sexual behaviour as a means of alleviating symptoms through distraction or self-soothing", exacerbating the problem of pornographic use and negatively impacting our mental health in response.[186]

This is supported by a separate study in *Psychology of Addictive Behaviours*, finding frequent pornography use was correlated to motives such as stress reduction, emotional distraction or suppression and boredom avoidance.[187] And yet, these methods are futile.

A recent study in *Psychology of Men & Masculinities* found that even if the motive were to reduce stress, porn can erode consumer autonomy, underpinning problematic use.[188] And it's not surprising.

According to *JAMA Psychiatry,* the consumption of porn, "even on a nonaddicted level, may have an impact on brain structure and function", with hours of pornography use correlating to a "significant negative association between reported pornography hours per week and gray matter volume" in the brain, causing "intense-stimulation of the reward system" and leading to "a higher need for external stimulation of the reward system and a tendency to search for novel and more extreme sexual material."[189]

While porn continues to function as a way of soothing the impact of mental health issues, it also makes it harder to stop consuming.

As with social media, porn exaggerates the problems we experience through the promise of an escape which further entrenches these problems.

The mainstreaming of pornography among younger age groups and its acceptance in the population as a whole, has elevated porn from an illicit, occasional activity to an escape of choice.

In society-on-demand, not only can we choose who we interact with, but we can also choose our sexual experience on-demand: and this has major implications, including in the sexualisation of others.

As Naomi Wolf put it in 2013:

> *For most of human history, erotic images have been reflections of, or celebrations of, or substitutes for, real naked women. For the first time in human history, the images' power and allure have supplanted that of real naked women. Today, real naked women are just bad porn.[190]*

And isn't this applicable to all areas of society-on-demand?

The nature of reality online and its dilution of the reality at hand means that porn – just like social media – becomes preferential: the favourable choice. Not the reality of our physical society – of our bodies and in person experience – but the fiction of our online selves.

Given the scale and pervasiveness of pornography and how easy it is to find (even by accident), what's the solution?

We've already explored the inability of parents to control device use or impose content blockers.

Once again, it's left to government to pick up the pieces and – once again – the government refuses to do so.

In 2019, plans were made to introduce age verification checks on porn sites, preventing under 18s from access. But the plan was scrapped, despite spending £2m on implementing a system which could, according to The Guardian, "be circumvented in less than two minutes using a simple Google search."[191]

And yet, despite these circumventions, other countries have succeeded in using government to regulate the Online.

In 2021, Germany successfully banned three Cyprus-based porn sites,[192] with France making similar moves to ban the five biggest sites in the country for their refusal to implement age verification checks.[193]

The UK's *Online Safety Bill* will – despite initial objections – finally introduce age-checks on pornographic content. This will also apply to social media platforms not currently blocking pornographic content, such as Twitter and Reddit.[194] Whether they will, once again, be dropped, we'll have to wait and see.[195]

Governments can – and often do – ban certain sites from operation, imposing rules on access. Porn seems like an easy place to start and yet, given that porn is viewed as acceptable by the public (not least widely engaged with), concerns over privacy and freedom seem to trump the restriction of access, as if an activity carried out online should not be subject to the same ID checks as buying a magazine.

This further exemplifies the problem we face: the perception of the internet as its own society; enabling behaviour which would not ordinarily occur in person, as if the internet should be a place without restriction, due to data privacy. The truth is, data can be protected when implementing age verification checks, we have the technology to achieve it and, even if we didn't, where's our data protection when we show our ID in a shop? These double standards are emblematic of society-on-demand.

Those opposed to such checks include Iain Corby of the Age Verification Providers Association, who claimed if the check was poorly enforced, "You stop going to PornHub, then you go to XHamster, then you go to the next down the list. Whatever you think of those sites they do tend to have some standards. You are driving people to sketchier sites".[196]

The normalisation of porn has become so entrenched that sites like Pornhub – forced to remove at least 10.6 million user-generated videos (the vast majority of its content) due to the presence of "rape, incest, child sexual abuse, forced/coerced/secretly filmed sex acts" and "racist, misogynist, violent themes" [197] – are now seen as the acceptable face of pornography: of "having some standards."

Of course, these issues must have been known to Pornhub; a company which presents itself as a bastion of equality and freedom, exploiting the anti-racism movement in the wake of George Floyd's murder, Tweeting:

> *Pornhub stands in solidarity against racism and social injustice. If you are able, we encourage you to give to organizations like @bailproject @BlackVisionsMN @MNFreedomFund @splcenter @NAACP*[198]

This Tweet was quickly identified by Fight The New Drug (an anti-porn campaign group) who responded by exposing a number of racist videos on Pornhub's website, such as *Black Slave Punished by White Master*, among others.[199] Not to be outdone, Pornhub pledged to donate "$100,000 to organizations actively fighting for equality", [200] allowing users to watch *Black Slave Girl Brutalized* with a clear conscience.[201]

Despite its flagrant hypocrisy, Pornhub was – once again – keen to portray its credentials as a progressive organisation, claiming it was "being targeted not because of our policies and how we compare to our peers, but because we are an adult content platform" brought down by "the same forces that have spent 50 years demonizing *Playboy*, the National Endowment for the Arts, sex education, LGBTQ rights, women's rights, and even the American Library Association. Today, it happens to be Pornhub."[202]

There aren't any words for this level of delusion; the idea that Pornhub and those like it have "some standards", unlike "sketchier sites", or that Pornhub is a kind of gimp-masked-vigilante for the LGBT community.

The Left often sees porn as inherently progressive. "My body, my choice", "sexual liberation" and "freedom of speech." And yet, this remains a convenient narrative for the porn industry which, clearly, wastes no opportunity to use progressive values as an excuse for its abuse; allowing the user to feel good about themselves while engaging in personally destructive and socially abusive behaviour.

The truth is, in portraying the pornography of anyone, let alone marginalised or systemically oppressed communities, people are, at best, commodified and, at worst, exploited and abused, with the viewer suffering serious consequences to the way they view others and themselves, impacting their relationships and mental health, not least through regressive and abusive acts against others.

In his brilliant book, *Empire of Illusion: The End of Literacy and the Triumph of Spectacle*, Chris Hedges claims that:

> *[Porn] is the disease of corporate and imperial power, control, force, and pain. It replaces empathy, eros, and compassion with the illusion that we are gods. Porn is the glittering façade, like the casinos and resorts in Las Vegas, like the rest of the fantasy that is America, of a culture seduced by death.*[203]

And yet, despite these damages, a bigger problem exists.

Everything Porn

Porn is not limited to sex. Porn is a feeling. A metaphor. As such, it's almost impossible to avoid. Even if we manage to avoid *actual* porn, it is now increasingly difficult to escape the pornographic, consumer culture in which we live.

In a world where communication is achieved through emojis and gifs, emojis have developed their own implicit meanings, where a well-placed aubergine creates the same excitement as a dick pic.

If something as innocuous as an emoji can be pornographic then we have to accept that anything can, and often is.

"Food porn", "travel porn", "book porn" and "insert-favourite-product-here-porn". There's a disturbing trend, championed on social media, to label whatever we see (whether it's a rustic display of apple tarts, a perfectly curated bookshelf or a cocktail shimmer by a sun-bathed pool), as "Porn."

We've lost the vocabulary to articulate the excessive nature of what we see and, importantly, how we feel.

The level of exposure to visual stimuli on social media – through sheer quantity and immediacy – evokes an emotional response which cannot be replicated offline.

The platforms we use encourage content presented as real, created by "people like us" (i.e., finitely resourced, non-famous users), adding to a sense of possibility and allowing us to long for things we might never be able to achieve. This illusion of reality creates a myth of access far greater than a magazine ever could.

How do we express this level of desire and accessibility? We label it with one of the few things that evokes a visceral response in today's society: "Porn."

"Everything porn" is an expression of consumerism; our inability to articulate the feelings and impulses driven by the matrix of material things. In a society based on desire, lust trumps all.

But this lust is not, as we've seen, limited to sex.

"Explicit content" should now include other things we've labelled illicit: material and experiential desire for products, fashion, food, holidays; anything and everything to which we've assigned value. This is all explicit: and impossible to escape.

We're caught in a web of being told what to want and need. We're bombarded with images designed to evoke an emotional response. We're so used to visual expression that we've lost the ability to think and express ourselves in any other way. Combine this with a literacy crisis, and self-expression becomes a mirror for the dominant culture: pornographic consumerism.

And in this context, a context of incessant image and insatiable desire; a society of "everything porn:" we're told we can be anything and do whatever we want. But there are two problems with this.

First, we're not things and, second, "being ourselves" isn't an option. There's no infinite spectrum on which to forge our own path: our paths are laid before us.

Social media, the best expression of this, promises a space to be ourselves, when its very purpose – its entire design – is to fit us into narrow, materialist ideals, driven by the idols of capital.

On social media, porn evolves from a feeling to a lifestyle.

"Hardcore" and "softcore" – used to define a pornographic expectation – have instead become a suffix for genres encapsulating the narrow and materialistic ideals (the choices laid before us) to "truly express ourselves." "Core" is a summary – a subgenre – for aesthetic. Just as everything has a "porn", everything has a "core."

"Cottagecore", "Gamecore", "Nostalgiacore", "Pastelcore" – even "Dadcore" – to name a few. But the "cores" don't end here.

Fashion trends have now imagined "Dystopiacore", otherwise known as "Apocalypsecore", mirroring "fashion originally popularised by military use" to reflect a "durable, self-contained, sustainable image." [204]

Dystopiacore has been said to "take inspiration from dark cinema fantasies such as The Matrix Resurrections and Dune." [205]

The problem is this: when everything is an aesthetic, meaning dies.

Art, intellect and creative ideas are not simply reduced to material things: they're not understood in the first place.

If we remain captive to the spectacle of the aesthetic, then the aesthetic is all we see.

Dystopiacore can pretend it's intrinsically meaningful; that it proves a wider artistic point. In reality, it's just another empty shell for the hollow ideology of materialism. Instead, Dystopiacore with meaning would be a McDonald's uniform, a prison garb or – to invoke *The Matrix* once more: a suit and tie.

The presentation of a core is nothing more than the admission that we lack what we're presenting; that our appearance demonstrates an idea we're incapable of actually forming. It is – instead of the presentation of who we are or what we believe – instead of the presentation of an idea (like Superman and Batman) – it is a presentation of irrelevance.

At least Goblincore has the self-awareness to be meaningless. And this should be how all cores function: an admission of meaningless aesthetics, wrapped in the delusion of self-expression.

And yet the oppression of the aesthetic doesn't stop at philosophy: today, the aesthetic oppresses aesthetic endeavours.

Instagram's 2022 Trend Report predicted that "alt-fashion (think Goth, Dark Academia, Goblincore, etc)" will "reach its peak as people spend more time together IRL [in real life]."[206]

The way we communicate has become so inept that aesthetics themselves have become a mode of communication. In a world where feelings are all we have and experience; where critical thought, communication and articulation have all but died: aesthetics are the softcore version of our pornographic culture.

And yet, porn is not just cultural expression or a pervasive feeling. It is also de facto everywhere in other forms of entertainment.

Pornography in the Mainstream

If we thought pornography *as* pop culture was damaging enough, then we'd misunderstand the nature of pornography.

Sexually explicit content is not restricted to pornography or even TV shows and movies, as we saw through *QuoDB*. Cardi B's *Wet-Ass Pussy*, Rihanna's *S&M* and *Anaconda* by Nicki Minaj exemplify a culture within the music industry where sex is seen as fair game – even a source of empowerment and celebration.

The problem is that regardless of how liberated the artist feels, the medium is, almost always, the message.

Asked about the controversy surrounding *WAP*, Cardi B dismissed concerns, claiming, "Everybody got a little freak inside them, you know? Every single person. Everybody gets horny, everybody gets a little tingle down there, you know what I'm saying. Just embrace it. Don't be scared about it."[207]

But if *WAP* is a celebration of sexuality, what kind of sexuality is celebrated?

With lyrics like, "He bought a phone just for pictures of this wet-ass pussy", "Put this pussy right in your face" and "I wanna gag, I wanna choke",[208] the song is a library of pornographic tropes which the audience is encouraged to embrace. What feels liberating for Cardi B appears abusive and damaging to others.

In response to these criticisms, Cardi B Tweeted:

I don't make music for kids I make music for adults. Parents are responsible on what their children listen too or see. I'm a very sexual person but not around my child just like every other parent should be.[209]

And yet, when the negative effects of porn have been well established, when *WAP* is available even on YouTube and when 60% of 11 to 13 year olds exposed to pornographic content are exposed against their wishes:[210] what are the chances of children discovering *WAP* through social media or other platforms, where they can view these videos without restriction and where the artists themselves have an online presence to promote their work?

We're often told to "take responsibility" for our actions. And yet, when our actions are inseparable from the material we see; when the material we see is pervasive and, in most cases, unavoidable, either through cultural reference or online presence: "taking responsibility" is impossible. In society-on-demand, content finds a way to be seen by millions of people who had no intention of seeing it.

And yet, sexual liberation isn't the only "reason" for pornography in music.

In response to *Anaconda*, a song about "fat asses" and shot like a porn film, Minaj dismissed the whole thing as a joke:

> *I wanted to create a song that embraced curvy women. I wanted to be sexual but be playful with it. And I wanted it to be so melodic that even if you don't understand English you could still go along with the melody and you would have no idea about all the raunchy shit I'm saying—I get a kick out of that. It was simple to write. I just created the melody and then I let the words happen. I started laughing when I said, "Boy toy named Troy." [Laughs.] That whole song, I was just being dumb. It was a joke.*[211]

The cost of these jokes is well-documented.

Just like *WAP; Anaconda* and *S&M* remain available on YouTube as accessible pop culture, with *Anaconda* surpassing a billion views on Nicki Minaj's official channel alone and *WAP* reaching almost half a billion in just eighteen months.

Despite this, a recent study found that sexual objectification and depicted sexuality in music videos remained steady between 1995 and 2016, although "ambiguous sexual expression, including sexual gestures, sexual poses, and sexual facial expressions, did increase over time", with female artists more often portrayed as sexually objectified than men, who were more likely to objectify others.[212] And this barely touches the surface.

A 2018 study analysing the effects of "exposure to sexually objectifying music videos" and their impact on "subsequent gazing behaviour", a clear link is made between exposure to "sexually objectifying" music videos and the objectification of "ideal size" women, even if they were fully dressed, and that "exposure to objectifying media has direct negative effects on women (and men)", which "can foster an objectifying gaze toward other women."[213]

Additionally, a study in the *Journal of Broadcasting and Electronic Media* analysing the "effects of sexually objectifying music videos on college men's sexual beliefs", found clear links between viewing "music videos of highly objectified female artists" and "more adversarial sexual beliefs, more acceptance of interpersonal violence, and, at a level of marginal significance, more negative attitudes about sexual harassment than participants assigned to low-sexual objectifying music videos by the same female artists."[214]

In a world where access to sexually explicit music is significantly easier through smartphones and social media, and when sexually explicit music is accepted as pop culture (*WAP* spent three weeks as the UK's *Number One*),[215] the normalisation of porn is accepted in the mainstream, even outside the specific realm of "actual" porn. Significant elements of the music industry support the objectification of women as the acceptable face of porn in pop culture, making the consumption of "actual" pornography more acceptable.

This impacts not just mental health and social cohesion, but the objectification of women through the objectifying gaze, itself directly influenced by exposure to sexual objectification in digital entertainment.

Of course, music isn't the only culprit. Perhaps the most obvious place to start is reality TV.

Shows claiming to promote relationships over sex, like ITV's *Love Island*, further exemplify the pornification of pop culture. And yet, this is perhaps best demonstrated by Netflix's *Too Hot To Handle*, a show where the entertainment isn't, we're told, for contestants to have sex but, expressly, to watch them *not* have sex.

The show is hosted by a virtual assistant which arranges dates and workshops, "spying" on contestants to see if they've broken the rules (i.e., if they've engaged in sexual activity).

If a contestant breaks the rules, the $200,000 prize money is reduced by varying amounts, depending on the level of activity (for example, kissing carries lower punishments, sex carries higher punishments).

Season three's winning couple received $45,000 each after the contestants lost $110,000 – over half the original prize money – through rule breaking. This included winning contestant, Harry, who lost $4,000 for "self-gratification."[216]

The show claims to encourage "deeper emotional connections",[217] but with episodes like, *Two's Company, Three's a ... Threesome,*[218] *Lust or Bust*[219] and *C**kblocked by a Cone,*[220] this is clearly secondary.

Too Hot To Handle is much less about not having sex than it is about the expectation of failure; of irrepressible desire in a cauldron of bikinis and ripped bodies. And therein lies the entertainment. The show allows its audience to achieve all the excitement of sex in the presumption that, at some point, resistance will be futile, the contestants will break the rules and – even if they're not breaking the rules – the audience can enjoy the sexual tension and partial nudity stemming from these rules.

And so we live in a society where sex is inextricably linked to entertainment, where producers feel not only encouraged – but empowered – to include sex as a fundamental part of digital entertainment.

If studios wished to establish meaningful connections, they wouldn't require contestants to look like models, dress them in thongs, play licentious sex games or elevate sexual tension.

Game of Thrones, the most watched TV show in history,[221] displays pornographic and abusive content in dozens of episodes. Of course, *GoT* is based on books where these things occur routinely: but it exemplifies the success of sex on TV, giving rise to shows such as *Black Sails*, *Westworld* and *Outlander*; each complete with a heavy dose of gratuitous sex and nudity.

In this context, Hulu's mini-series, *Pam and Tommy*[222] – a show about the release of a stolen sex tape (in today's language, "Revenge Porn") – is an obvious series to produce.

The involvement of A-List actors Lily James, Sebastian Stan and Seth Rogen, alongside renowned screen writer, Robert Siegel, presumes a large audience.

How could it not? A film about the world's most infamous sex tape with an all-star cast to boot.

And yet, Pamela Anderson was not involved.

Siegel and James both attempted to contact her to "be involved" in the production, presumably in the interest of fairness and accuracy, allowing her to share her perspective and tell her story. Anderson didn't reply, so Hollywood did what it did best and produced the show anyway, without her blessing.[223]

While the show portrayed the harassment, abuse and suffering she experienced within a wider critique of systemic misogyny and objectification; the show also legitimised porn by making a clear distinction between the exploitation of Anderson and Lee's relationship, due to their lack of consent in the tape's release, versus the pornography industry itself, where actors agree to their own exploitation.

Whatever the overall message of the series, exploiting the relationships of others without their consent is just a normal part of society: and this is exactly what Hulu achieved in publishing the series without Anderson's blessing.

Of course, a society that uses sex to boost ratings is a society which becomes over-sexualised, where objectification is normal and exposure is expected. To criticise this is to be dismissed as prudish or being told to, "Grow-up, it's only a boob!" To criticise porn is to be an enemy of men and women: against the normalcy of exploitation by men and the "freedom" of women to make their own choices and objectify themselves.

Like other aspects of digital entertainment, the problem is circular, with content driving consumption and consumption driving content.

Railing against the injustices of objectification is fundamental to the political challenges we face. And yet, it's increasingly difficult to accomplish. The forces of a sexually exploitative and objectifying media, combined with immediate and personal access through smartphones and a society which, after decades of normalisation, accepts these things as not just important, but liberating; is a society that's guaranteed to fail when asked to see others as human beings, not objects.

Porn – like social media – is a tool which suits the government; a device to placate, control and separate, to silo relationships and fundamentally change the nature of what a relationship is; from something strong and unconditional to something weak, conditional and apathetic.

And yet, when a Tory MP watches porn on their phone – in the middle of the House of Commons, surrounded by other MPs[224] – the response is not, "we have a porn epidemic, smartphones have turned this into a crisis, we need serious reform." Instead, it's platitudes about how everyone watches it, but it should remain "private."

Watch as much porn as you like. Objectify to your heart's content. Revel in the abuse of others: just don't do it near me.

Once again, the duplicity of society-on-demand – that we can separate our lives online from our lives in person, is both delusional and pathetic. The impact of society-on-demand is long-lasting. It affects us long after engagement, whether it's social media, porn, football, direct messaging or binge-watching TV shows. As we've seen, these effects, when damaging to our selves, are inherently damaging to others; with millions of people hooked on a life of damaging consumption, tearing apart not just our own lives, but the fabric of an already unjust, fatigued and abusive society.

Under these circumstances – where consumption is presumed, not challenged – we are asked to both respect and value others, online and in person, *except* in pornography, where it's both, a. accepted we'll watch it and, b. understood that objectification is our main source of gratification.

Again, the hypocrisy of society-on-demand is not just a moral failure: it's logistically absurd.

"Objectify others, rewire your brains and suffer, *but be a gentleman and respect women.*"

Needless to say, while society suffers, government benefits. Society enjoys pornography, pornography placates society through sexual gratification, so society embraces it, allowing us to objectify others, breaking social relations, dehumanising ourselves and each other. This makes political and social change even harder to achieve, as if we weren't labouring enough.

And we're not done yet. Before looking to the future, there remains a need to explore digital entertainment in general; the background noise of society-on-demand; the bread and butter of the problems we face: film, TV and on-demand streaming.

DIGITAL ENTERTAINMENT

I need more than chocolate, and for that matter I need more than vanilla. I believe that we need freedom, and choice when it comes to our ice cream, and that, Joey Naylor; that is the definition of liberty.

Nick Naylor, Thank You For Smoking.[225]

Thinking back to the *Carousel of Progress*, the introduction of the TV and radio brought an immensity of choice, transforming life at home from the use of our own resources as entertainment (reading books, playing games, conversation), to sitting in front of the TV as "something to do after you come home."

And yet, despite the fundamental changes this "progress" introduced – in our own lives and society at-large – they remained limited in scope. There was a schedule, a limited selection of options and, through this, a commonality imposed by these limits.

For example, it simply wasn't possible for one household to watch one thing while the other watched something else, the next one something else, and so on; nor could anyone sit and plough through a year's worth of content. Families couldn't sit together in separate modes of entertainment or interest, as we saw with the smartphone and, if they did, they were restricted to books, magazines, drawing, writing, board games or socialisation; manual tasks through which we remained accessible and available to others, not plugged-in to society-on-demand.

Indeed, in the 1950s, TV broadcasts were forced to break for a full hour between 6 and 7pm. Known as the "Toddler's Truce", this break allowed children to get ready for bed, spending at least an hour away from the screen before going to sleep, something we now view as a healthy thing to do. This hour also ensured families were present for each other in the last moments of their child's day, with not even adult programming available during this hour. The TV was blank.

In the 50s, TV was only allowed to broadcast a maximum of 12 hours on a weekday, 8 hours on a Saturday and 7 and three quarter hours on a Sunday (with no Children's programming between 2pm and 4pm).

Guardian journalist, Benjie Goodhart, refers to this as "draconian", questioning the Postmaster General, Herbrand Sackville (whose brief included oversight of telecoms and broadcasting), who supported these measures "in spite of his seemingly progressive politics".

The idea that progressives should support freedom of choice at all costs simply because we enjoy what's available, is a modern phenomenon; one no doubt enabled and encouraged by the companies wihch benefit from these inventions and services, no matter how damaging they might be.

Goodhart finishes by claiming, "Remarkably, the fabric of the nation remained intact in spite of TV now transmitting between 6pm and 7pm at night."[226]

But did it?

In 1972, Christopher Chataway, as Minister for Posts and Telecommunications (the reformed role of Postmaster General) lifted all restrictions on broadcast hours, signalling the beginning of a new era: limitless digital entertainment.[227]

Fifty years later, when we spend almost 6 hours a day watching video content and when children suffer mental health crises from too much screen time: claiming "the fabric of the nation remained intact" is not only wrong: it's immoral. As we've seen, parents *do* struggle to limit screen time for their kids and are often unable to prevent the consumption of harmful content, incapable of regulating even their own screen time.

Just like the Christmas TV guide, an increasing relic of the past and the last of the scheduling era, broadcast TV has been fundamentally compromised by the rise of on-demand video. Live TV itself is in radical decline, accounting for just 61% of total watch time in 2020, down 6% from 2019. This is even more apparent when split between age groups, with 16 to 34 year olds watching just 65 minutes of broadcast TV a day (less than a quarter of their total screen time), versus 162 minutes – more than an hour and a half more – of the adult population as a whole.[228]

And yet, as if limitless TV wasn't enough to quench our thirst, we now frolic in a stream of on-demand video. No longer able to wait for a schedule, we demand everything now: wherever, whenever and however we want.

The Burden of Choice

In *Thank You For Smoking*, protagonist Nick Naylor equates our ability to choose with freedom. To be stuck with vanilla or chocolate ice cream is not a choice. Rather, it is to have access to both, to be able to choose, demonstrating freedom and liberty.[229]

And yet, there is another choice: the freedom to choose nothing.

As I've argued throughout this book, the problem isn't choosing "better" aspects of the problems we face (Liverpool vs. Chelsea, the female vs. the male gaze or Twitter vs. Facebook): it's about recognising that football, pornography and social media – through the prism and industry of digital entertainment – have coalesced into the disarming of physical society and, with it, the fracturing of in person relationships and the demise of political and social solidarity; replaced by the apathy and division of society-on-demand. Simply choosing different aspects of this society will not solve the problem of its existence; just as Dunhill vs. Marlboro will not solve the problem of smoking.

Just like the tobacco lobby, which presents the freedom to smoke as a legitimate choice, digital entertainment takes a similar approach. And yet, the digital entertainment industry has imposed a level of choice which, rather than giving us the freedom to choose whether to consume or not, has instead imposed the illusion that we *have to consume something*.

Unlike the tobacco industry, which simply wants to exist *as* a choice, the digital entertainment industry wants us to take consumption for granted; that we will – due to its ubiquity – inevitably indulge, given how pervasive it is.

This level of choice – not just of what's available but in *where* and *when* it's available – has clobbered us with the illusion that, "Well, if there's so much here, there must be *something* worth watching!" And so we spend thirty minutes choosing what to watch before deciding on something we've seen before; good enough to placate us but bad enough to continue the search later. Of course, if all else fails, there's always the Netflix *Play Something* feature,[230] a phrase one exclamation mark away from the panic it's designed to address. But is this level of choice really that bad?

Thanks to Spotify and YouTube Music, we no longer have to suffer the iniquities of the radio, a choice between Adele, Sam Smith and Ed Sheeran. The same can be said for streaming services.

And yet, we come back to the problematic nature of these platforms and the industry in its current form: instead of having a set number of programmes, channels, movies and bands, making it easier to say "no" and restricting our time spent watching or listening to things we don't actually care for, we are instead dominated by the omnipresence of the digital entertainment industry; immediately accessible, anywhere, at any time.

Instead of a limited, scheduled availability of digital entertainment, allowing us to use our time and energy better, improving our mental health and relationships with others; we instead suffer relentless choice and access.

This immediacy is not a requirement to access diverse content. We've always been able to access films and musicians not scheduled on the TV or radio, without a plethora of other choices: it just meant that we had to pay for specific pieces of content (a specific movie at Blockbuster or a specific album at the record store; choices which remain, incidentally, today, when the streaming services available refuse to platform the show or movie we want to watch, forcing us to purchase specific titles as digital copies or physical products on an individual basis).

There's a poetry to subjecting ourselves to the dominant narrative; a humility we know only when we suffer the scourge of what's popular.

Today, the cultural pressure to have watched "X" show (or at least know something about it in order to engage in a discussion) is palpable, leading us to not only watch what we want in our own time, but also what everyone else is watching, to remain relevant and avoid the derision of colleagues, becoming a kind of social pariah ("How have you not seen *Squid Game*?!")

And yet, in April 2021, streaming services accounted for 115,000 hours of content in the UK alone. It's simply not possible to stay up to date with this much content.[231]

The sheer volume and convenience of digital entertainment has accelerated a society already in decline to a society which is, finally, ending.

The existence of a physical, human society – of community and solidarity – is jeopardised because of our need to remain plugged-in. The sharing of digital content has resulted in almost no shared physical existence. We go to the same places, yet we go with headphones in our ears. We ride the same transport, yet we stare at our phones. We see our friends and family, but are too preoccupied with our followers on social media or the digital versions of others. Our online selves have subverted our in person lives.

The aim of digital entertainment shouldn't be to accommodate all tastes in monolithic, time-consuming services. Rather, it should be to improve the quality of content and equality of access, scheduled at a particular time, like a traditional TV show or even a football match. Imposing fixed scheduling would allow us to plan our lives around content, rather than content planning our lives: far from a perfect solution, but a better one than the status quo, where content *is* our lives.

Just as we need a ticket for a concert or an event, this principle should apply to online entertainment. This means limited and scheduled social media posts, YouTube videos, Netflix and Prime releases, etc. It also means a drastic reduction in the number of shows produced and platformed.

Of course, we have the ability to treat our digital media consumption with this level of discipline. But, hard as we try, we seem unable to; the social pressure to stay up to date beating us into submission once more. Like quitting smoking, we're required to be disciplined; to engage in a battle for our will.

When we can watch whatever we want, whenever we want, and when there's an expectation that if we refresh the page every few seconds, something interesting enough for us to waste our time will appear; then we have little room for anything else, whether that's doing nothing and sitting with our thoughts or broadening ourselves through work or leisure of value and fulfilment.

Today, we're in a permanent state of consumption; paralysing our humanity, rotting our brains and damaging our perception. Our talents remain hidden, our skills, suppressed. Scroll, refresh, scroll, refresh. The rhythm of our lives.

The Switch

So what's the solution?

It may sound like broadcast television is the ideal solution to our problems: scheduled, free and limited.

The BBC, long seen as a high-quality, informative and value-for-money service, away from the influence of advertisers is, on paper, a model example. Instead, it plays a crucial role in the placation and subservience of the public, funded by an involuntary license fee of more than £13 a month, far higher than the average streaming service, without the production value and, critically, without choice.

For millions of people, £159 a year is unaffordable. And yet, even if it were funded through a progressive tax, excluding the poorest households, the BBC's basic problem would remain: it is, generally, awful.

While the institution of the BBC is fundamentally important (having the potential to be a neutral, independent, high-quality organisation; able choose its own stories, hold government to account, display and promote the best of British and global culture while providing opportunities to those who would otherwise have none): its delivery is largely woeful.

Instead of living up to its purpose of providing an impartial, high-quality service, the BBC, in practice, upholds the political status quo, patronising its audience; producing shows like *Strictly Come Dancing, EastEnders*

111

and *Match of the Day*. Shows like *Killing Eve*, *The Bill*, *Line of Duty*, *Bodyguard* and *Silent Witness*, among others, glorify policing as a force for good against the darkness of serial killers, rapists and other elusive threats to society, keeping the public hooked on the entertainment of brutality (just as execution and torture served as both entertainment and warning, hundreds of years ago), magnifying the threat we face and asking the public to trust in the Police, whose corrupt officers are never the result of policing: just bad apples.

To provide a scale of the problem, *Line of Duty* and *Bodyguard* were watched an average 13 million times, with the perennial *Strictly* at 12.5 million; shows defending what we're told is an imperfect but critical establishment apparatus beyond the scope of even moderate change or, in the case of *Strictly*, being told not to worry, because a coalition of celebrities, flashing lights and raunchiness is there to comfort us: so sit down, shut up and consume.[232] [233]

These shows are propaganda for the status quo masked as entertainment. And while *BBC News*, *Question Time*, *Newsnight* and others serve to maintain the status quo in plain sight, the BBC relies far more on the millions of people who skip reality and, instead, consume the trash they're served at 7pm on a Sunday night.

These are cultural monoliths, created, promoted and freely accessed for the sole purpose of dominating the town square (the office space, the pub, the kitchen table). Instead of discussing anything of value, we discuss the performance of celebrities on *Strictly*, the incestuous rape of an *EastEnders* character or the Mole in the police force.

Of course, there's nothing wrong with the town square in principle: we need points of commonality for socialisation; a bare minimum to cope in social environments and build relationships. But when these minimums become all that matters, leaving no room for further divergence; when we remain prisoners of the lowest common denominator: there's a systemic and fundamental failure of culture: and a failure of culture is a failure of our humanity.

The BBC's purpose – like that of Netflix, Disney+ and Amazon Prime – is to placate, distract and promote meaningless, emotionally manipulative content. That doesn't mean everything's bad. Make enough programmes and you can expect at least some of them to be good. But for every *Planet Earth* there's a *Doctor Who*; for every *Borgen*, an *EastEnders*; for every *Taboo*, a *Weakest Link*.

And, if people *do* want to check the news or engage with current events, then no problem, because all these shows serve the same purpose: to keep us ignorant and intellectually limited under the guise of public service and neutrality.

The O'Reilly Factor – a former Fox News show – prepared its viewers by proclaiming, "Caution! You are about to enter the No Spin Zone",[234] before (of course) spinning even more than it might otherwise do, with the proclamation of "no spin" permitting an even greater amount of disinformation.

The BBC's neutrality functions the same way: it's just smart enough to understand subtlety is more powerful than blatant propaganda.

Even *Match of the Day*, a widely consumed show watched by 60% of the public,[235] a show which can pay its host £1.3 million,[236] only exists to ensure the masses receive their weekly dose of sport before the work week begins (a week we can spend talking about football, rather than anything important).

And so when its host, Gary Lineker, defends the BBC as "the most treasured of national treasures",[237] we should think two things:

First, of course he does. He earns millions from license-fee payers and, second, "the most treasured?"

To Lineker, and no doubt others, the BBC occupies the same space as the NHS. This isn't an accident.

While Lineker isn't responsible for the mirage of digital entertainment, he is a symptom of its self-professed relevance and necessity; to present the escape as more important than the reality we're escaping from.

Instead, we need to see the escape as something we're forced to endure; not something we're supposed to enjoy, crucial to coping with the rest of our lives in physical space.

Like our heroes in *The Good Place*, nothing is often better than the alleged positives we're presented with.

And yet, for the BBC in particular, we've now reached a point where the dominance of digital entertainment has become so entrenched that the government feels able to scrap the license fee entirely, ending the current funding model in just a few years' time, relying instead on private subscription services such as Netflix to make up the entertainment gap.[238]

In the context of society-on-demand, there are only upsides to hammering the BBC: the government gets to remove an organisation with regular politics and news coverage, and instead leave its citizens in the hands of private streaming services; increasing our reliance on society-on-demand and the apathy both essential to – and demanded by – its existence. For the government, there's no downside, allowing the public to follow the United States down the road of weak broadcast networks, resulting in further political disengagement, shifting the sphere of politics and information further to the Right through social media.

Despite its problems, the BBC is, in many ways, a last stand against the complete trivialisation of all things; forcing us to look at a bigger, wider world, regardless of how politically biased and condescending it might be.

The Death of the Event

The rise of digital entertainment and the decline of public space has made instant access not only possible, but preferable; having become so used to the immediacy and availability of all things (with the right subscription service) that we're no longer living *just* with the end of mystery, with everything able to be instantly known and shown: but with the death of the event itself.

The cinematic event no longer whelms us. Concerts no longer transcend us. Nature no longer moves us. The Moment is no longer allowed to live in itself.

The presence of our phones – the impossible brightness of a retina-burning screen or the pollution of an ocean of LCDs, the arrogant beam of an LED torch – is a negation of the Moment; living not in the present, but in the future, evidence for later when we can – once more – escape into the past. Today, memory is something we prefer to keep on an SD card: and the screen is a framing device for the reality we live.

Why is this important?

There's no doubt the visual evidence of our lives matters, exemplifying our experience and allowing us to see, in the future (and with precision), the life we lived. But this is not the same as memory.

A recording cannot replicate our experience because our experience was instead *the act of recording what we were supposed to experience*. The moment we clicked record was the moment we stepped out of our lives.

Would recording our own marriage proposal make the moment better? Would the surprise of a child's first steps – their first words – be greater spent fumbling for our phones?

Chances are, romance would die; elation would end; defeated in our attempt to preserve the moment through a camera, rather than our own experience. We've allowed the ubiquity of the camera to replace our own experience, prioritising instead the external preservation of the image over the tapestry of our own minds.

We need the time and space to be in our own moments, to live our own lives. The danger, as we've seen throughout this book, is that society-on-demand removes not only the possibility of experience through time spent online, but also the potential for memory itself.

The irony, of course, is that when we choose to document our lives for nostalgia's sake, we ruin both nostalgia and memory; preventing us from experiencing what might have been worth remembering in the first place, depriving us of the nostalgia we seek. This leaves us without an escape, with our lived experience forming part of the digital entertainment infrastructure; of physical reality itself a seamless part of the user-generated-content of our lives; leaving even our own existence and memory of it forsaken, swallowed by the scourge of society-on-demand.

So far, we've seen how the rise of digital entertainment, its immediacy and variety, has birthed a culture of continuous consumption. The ubiquity of the smartphone has fundamentally damaged society and young people, in particular, for whom digital engagement has replaced physical reality, compromising their mental health, identity and relationships. We've seen how pornography has enabled us to further objectify others, causing serious mental health problems and the perception of others as mere objects, and how this objectification has become a continuous presence in our culture. We've seen how on-demand streaming and meaningless entertainment through propaganda and weak content has imposed itself as a necessary foundation of our lives. We've seen how the subversion of political change through the false hope of football has empowered a culture of short-termism, living day by day and week by week in the absence of further meaning and, through this, we've seen how our failure to deliver change is a direct consequence of the apathy generated by this "progress" and how the Left continues to see these problems as part of the solution; refusing to acknowledge the division, dysfunction and diversion they impose.

But what's next?

Given the scale of the damage to individuals, society and political change – not even two decades into the smartphone revolution – our trajectory is clear: and it's not good.

And yet, if society-on-demand is to truly solidify itself as our society of choice, it needs to show it can operate on a similar level to its physical enabler. For that, it needs its own means of production. It needs financial relevance. The Online must transform itself from a place we continue to see as largely free to a place where we spend most of our disposable income.

Today, our financial interests remain fixed in physical reality.

While we continue to rent streaming services, most of the money we spend online is for goods we receive in person (books, groceries, tickets, etc). And while society-on-demand has excelled at replacing things which were already free or affordable (time, relationships, TV, movies, music, football), it has failed to establish its own value through its own products and experiences. With pornography, it's gone even further; taking something which cost money in person and transforming it into something which is, for the most part, free.

If the Online is to truly replace physical society, then this needs to be flipped, with the Online becoming the default location of our disposable income. It needs to generate its own products and experiences. In much the same way an apple can only be eaten in-person, the Online needs its own products to be consumed and experienced online. And for that, there's one illustration, in particular, which perfectly encapsulates society-on-demand and the direction we're headed: the NFT.

Capital's Endgame

The "Non-Fungible Token" allows us to purchase something we'll never physically possess. A "digital asset."

These assets can be purchased, copied, sold and reused by anyone using cryptocurrency. Multiple people can own the same NFT; be it an image, song or even a Tweet. NFTs do not need to be digital assets: they can also represent physical objects.

NFTs have been compared to collectibles, like baseball cards. But baseball cards are physical objects. The cards themselves aren't made of anything special. Their value is based on scarcity. The *appeal* of baseball cards, however, transcends financial gain: they're a way of expressing ourselves. For example, most collectors are fans of baseball. Stamp collectors enjoy the history their collections display. Collectibles are a way of socialising with friends and delving into the hobbies we love. And, as physical objects, we can tangibly engage with these interests, providing a physical connection to the things we enjoy.

NFTs are used same way. A buyer can share their NFT in the metaverse, displaying digital art on virtual walls or a virtual showcase. A song can be playing on a virtual radio through a VR headset and friends can hang out in the virtual home they've created. And yet, this is the only place their collections can reside: in digital form in a virtual space. They are not real. The buyer often receives nothing except "digital ownership."

And so, if you thought society-on-demand was bad enough, we've now entered a world where decorating the walls of our digital homes is a normal thing to do. Forget the housing crisis.

Because NFTs are inextricable from the digital realm, anything can be sold as an NFT. If the asset does not represent a physical object and is accessible even by non-owners (like most digital content), then we have to recognise that the NFT is nothing more than a duplication of physical assets; a monstrous blend of social media and a virtual stock market. To return to our previous analogy: NFTs are just baseball cards... without the cards.

Football clubs are already selling NFTs to supporters, allowing fans to "feel more connected and attached to their favorite football team."[239] Disney has also entered the NFT market, selling "Marvel Digital Comics" through *VeVe*, an app-based company selling digital collectibles, allowing buyers to display their collections in virtual (or augmented) reality, through their phones. For example, an issue of *Deadpool*, featuring "The first appearance of Blind Al!" is sold for $6.99, plus 8.5% in additional fees. The buyer can display the comic in VR and sell it later.[240] Meanwhile, purchasing the digital version of the same comic through Marvel, costs just $1.99.[241] We are now monetising the intangible; paying more for the "investment" rather than the experience of the thing itself (in this case, reading the comic).

To say the metaverse is yet to begin when we're already augmenting public space with digital assets and furnishing VR homes, would be dangerously optimistic. Instead, we're shuffling virtual deckchairs on the Titanic.

Already, through smartphones alone, we augment our realities with overlays of digital products; new sources of interaction through the relegation of the real world to a mere platform for the elevation of digital assets.

It's only a matter of time until film studios sell famous scenes as NFTs. Captain America wielding Mjölnir, Neo dodging bullets or "You had me at hello."

Porn actors could sell their bodies as NFTs, letting us not only objectify, but possess; allowing our lust to run its course from dehumanisation to full ownership.

A precedent for this has already been established, with Croation tennis player Oleksandra Oliynykova selling lifetime ownership to part of her right arm. The buyer can display whatever they want on her skin (for example, a tattoo) so long as it avoids extremist messaging, gambling, etc.[242] And, if you did wish to purchase the rights to her arm, you can rest assured that you can even "leave it blank – but you will know it's yours."[243]

In Season 2 of *The Boys*, a mutant named Gecko regenerates his own body. Naturally, he sells himself on the black market, allowing customers to mutilate him for their own pleasure. In one scene, we see him in a motel room getting his arm hacked off by an elated customer.[244]

While this is an extreme example, it's difficult to see how NFTs are any different. A customer pays for ownership of a body part and the seller may or may not let the "owner" do certain things with it.

But it gets worse.

As if objects weren't enough, Polish Influencer, Marta Rentel, has sold love – yes, *love* – as an NFT.

But this love isn't Marta Rentel's: it's *Marti Renti's*, the "online persona" of Marta Rentel.

"Coming from the parallel world where the internet is my stage," Renti claims that selling her digital love will allow her "to become digitally complete" by finding a buyer "who's crazy enough to travel with me to this infinite galaxy of digital emotions."[245]

And yet, despite digital love being the product of her online persona, Rentel has promised to have dinner with the buyer once the transaction is complete.[246]

So who goes on the date? Marta Rentel... or Marti Renti? If the "digital love" belongs to Marti Renti, how does the online persona present itself in person? How does the buyer own the emotion of a fake persona; a persona we're assured is not the same as the one meeting them for dinner? Of course, these aren't the concerns a buyer would have.

According to Renti, "Selling digital love is empowering for women because we can love without compromising our freedom and individuality,"[247] claiming that "even digital things must submit to the everlasting laws that never change."[248]

And yet, this freedom and individuality belongs to Rentel, who remains free to love whomever she wants; allowing the online persona of Renti to shoulder the burden of ownership. Designing the NFT around a digital persona allows Rentel to live without the consequence of her digital life. Not only does Rentel get to love whomever she likes, she could also (presumably) kill Renti by deleting her accounts, leaving the owner of her digital love a kind of "NFT Widow" (a status they could then sell as an NFT).

The sale of fake emotion through a fake persona earned Renti $250,000. And yet, given that Renti is the online persona, whose account does it go to?[249]

Fanadise, the company platforming Renti, has already advertised the sale of "hate", "hope" and "trust."[250]

Equating digital assets to the same status as physical objects is, clearly, insane. But this is exactly how they're seen.

Advertising Rentel's "First ever NFT Love!" Fanadise claims:

> By crafting my Digital Love (and other emotions) I'm only naming a thing that already exists but no one seems to notice. Physical love, platonic love and digital love may be different, but each one is real in the same way all our thoughts and feelings are. And digital means eternal - like for real. People are passing away but whatever remains - photographs, souvenirs, old letters - ignites the memories of those who're no longer with us. And what's now being digitized will stay with us till the end of the world.[251]

We are no longer dealing with the digitisation of physical assets, but with the digitisation of humanity itself.

To view digital love with the same reverence as love is to destroy love through commodification. All "love" requires is someone to sell it and someone to buy it. Of course, the desire to sell love is not love at all – just as the digital love of an online persona cannot exist (not least when they have no idea to whom this love is addressed). Love requires a target.

NFTs occupy the curious space of products without products. Their value exists because we've said it does. There are no external measures of their impact or importance.

And so. Not only do NFTs make almost no financial sense as a digital asset; they are uniquely dangerous: allowing us to assign financial value to things which should not be monetised: emotions, body parts – even relationships.

NFTs are seen as a way to express our support for and identity through other people; be they football clubs, artists, models and so on. The ownership of the NFT is a declaration of support and identity through financial investment.

While the seller of the NFT might also include a physical benefit (like a dinner date or advertising space on the human body); the general purpose of digital assets is to invest and align; not receive physical assets or experiences.

And this leads me to the crucial point: *NFTs would not be possible had we not already accepted the complete objectification of our selves.* Through society-on-demand, our objectification of each other, of nature – of the universe – can now reach its logical conclusion: the monetisation of everything.

Where capitalism succeeded in defining us by what we own and experience (making our joy dependent on what we earn and possess); today is the first time we can monetise not just the objects and experiences we desire: but desire itself. Our identity – our entire selves – can be expressed through financial means. The blockchain – where NFT ownership and transactions are recorded – is the ledger of our lives.

To see everything in financial terms; to reduce humankind to financial gain; to objectify, to debase, to despise. These are the forces behind slavery; the natural end game of capitalism. We can do whatever we want, without consequence: we're dealing with assets, not people.

And, while the blockchain allows us to voluntarily engage; the mindset of ownership and investment – to build a digital utopia from the wreck of our physical lives – is becoming personalised and mainstream, laying the groundwork for the metaverse.

When we reduce our humanity – not just our bodies, but our personalities – to a financial asset: we kill our selves.

We shall fight them on the Blockchains

In 2021, El Salvador became the first country to recognise Bitcoin – the world's largest cryptocurrency – as legal tender.[252] [253]

The law, introduced by Millennial President Nayib Bukele – "the coolest dictator in the world" [254] – was announced on Twitter while – at the same time – Bitcoin crashed, dropping 20% and wiping $3 million off one of the poorest countries in Latin America.[255] Six months later, things got even worse, with Bitcoin running at 22% less than the government paid for it, losing tens of millions of dollars.[256]

And yet, as of February 2022, Bukele showed no sign of correcting this.

The self-professed "CEO of El Salvador" has, instead, decided to launch a Bitcoin "Volcano Bond", raising one billion dollars, to create "Bitcoin City"; a giant mining facility at the base of a volcano, powered by geothermal energy.[257]

As a right-wing populist,[258] Bukele's desire to double-down on his mistakes is, seemingly, obligatory.

I don't say this to mock Bukele. Rather, for someone who ran for President via Facebook Live,[259] Bukele is one of a growing number of techno-centric elites who believe the latest tech can solve our problems and that governments can function through smartphones alone.

Following the invasion of Ukraine in February 2022, Ukraine's Deputy Minister of Digital Transformation announced a series of NFTs to bankroll the military, allowing buyers to own pieces of the war as digital assets. According to Bornyakov, the NFT collection would be "like a museum of the Russian-Ukrainian war."[260]

Of course, fighting with NFTs is like firing pictures of bullets or dressing wounds with Photoshop bandages: their only purpose is to raise capital and voice support for Ukrainian armed forces; a donation based on propaganda, not military necessity.

Whereas war bonds were issued to finance government debt, NFTs are purchased to finance mementos. There's no stake in the government; just patriotic gestures.

Ukraine has even launched its own cryptocurrency page, "the first-ever instance of a cryptocurrency exchange directly cooperating with a public financial entity to provide a conduit for crypto donations." [261] This shouldn't be a surprise.

Before the invasion, Ukraine was on its way to building a "state in a smartphone", allowing "100% of government services [to] be offered online."

Like Bukele, Ukraine's Digital Minister, Mykhailo Fedorov, sees Twitter as an "efficient tool" to "counter Russian military aggression" and "a smart and peaceful tool to destroy Russian economy".

According to the BBC, "At only 31, Fedorov has shaped his government role around his lifestyle – he lives through and on his mobile phone."[262]

The Democratisation of War

Two weeks before the invasion, Ukraine's President, Volodymyr Zelensky, launched "Diia City."

Powered by massive tax cuts and special employment laws, Diia was designed to make Ukraine "one of the largest IT hubs in Europe", tripling revenue and increasing the sector from 4% to 10% of GDP through a 25 year tax cut. Diia City would, according to Zelensky, become "a digital capital of the electronic state".

The "electronic state" – or the "state in a smartphone" – is backed by the top levels of the Ukrainian government.[263]

124

So when a brutal and unjust invasion occurs, and the response of the government is cryptocurrency, digital assets and social media, we should think two things:

First, it's not surprising. Governments – like the people they govern – are increasingly blinded by the power of the Online: becoming the default option for the execution of physical reality. This is especially the case in countries like El Salvador and Ukraine, where governments are led by younger people.

And yet, even the UK is looking at cryptocurrency, with the Chancellor claiming, "We want to see the [cryptocurrency] businesses of tomorrow – and the jobs they create – here in the UK, and by regulating effectively we can give them the confidence they need to think and invest long-term."[264]

The Royal Mint, at the request of the Treasury, is even launching its own NFT, making the UK "a hospitable place for crypto" to "attract investment [and] generate swathes of new jobs."[265]

Like El Salvador and Ukraine, this goes beyond regulation: it's active participation.

Second, the consequences of this are not adequately considered.

For example, what happens when people are invited to buy NFTs and donate cryptocurrency?

Thousands of new users are sucked in, NFTs and crypto become mainstream and the context of a "moral resistance" against invasion allows deeply unstable currencies and digital asset bubbles to become not reckless, but "cool." The popularity of these assets through the lens of moral impetus will increase, becoming a normal part of everyday life.

Like the absurdity of volcano-powered Bitcoin, we now have a political context to continue our leap into the End; a moral imperative to digitise everything.

Infrastructure

The race for a digital world is, as we saw earlier, exemplified by the reduction of public space and human engagement. With digital infrastructure offering cheaper alternatives to physical space and human relationships, the act of employing people or improving physical space is clearly more time consuming and expensive than distributing access via smartphone.

And that means poorer countries – or those emerging from the horrors of war – are less likely to invest in physical infrastructure, developing cheaper options instead. For countries struggling financially (and, in the wake of austerity and a global pandemic, who isn't?) the decision to return to a human-centred, physical society makes little financial sense, with the digital space offering a near endless supply of money and placation: an economy which thrives – and relies – on the inaction of its Subjects. Poorer nations like El Salvador and Ukraine have already taken this to extremes with cryptocurrency and the digital state, while the UK – among others – has used these crises as an excuse to power automation at the expense of jobs; digital entertainment instead of physical engagement and smartphones over physical space; depriving us of the humanity and solidarity we need. Accelerating the digital is to prioritise the digital economy at society's expense.

So long as the active participants of society-on-demand hold public office (a situation which could become more common as younger people enter politics), this is a problem which is only going to get worse.

In a few years, AR, VR and the digital economy will be our default. While today we check social media first thing in the morning, the future will demand continuous economic, as well as social, engagement. The reduction of public space will be empowered by its destruction, with AR overlays. Reality will be the stage for our digital lives.

Much like *Pokémon Go*, the smartphone game which uses augmented reality to catch digital Pokémon in physical space, we'll interact with the metaverse in society itself.

Physical space will become a staging-ground for digital assets. Just like the digital collectible, allowing the "owner" to view their asset in a virtual showroom or on a physical desk through augmented reality; we will engage with digital assets and even the digital presence of others within public space. Coffee shops will ensure they have enough space for virtual friends to meet their physical counterparts. Empty chairs will line cafes not for more customers, but for virtual attendees. The only thing keeping restaurants open will be the food. The social aspect will be all but dead, with people preferring the ease of meeting digitally, much like DMs are preferred to phone calls or in person meetings. Already, the aesthetic of the physical is to provide sufficient empty space through a minimalist design – like your local Apple store.

Just as we interact on Twitter and "meet" online, the metaverse will go further, allowing us to attend events and feel like we're in the same room – to "grab a drink" at the virtual bar – perhaps even take digital pictures of the virtual event we're attending, before selling them as NFTs.

This is not farfetched. On the contrary, this is exactly what's being planned and, steadily, implemented; not just by *Meta*, but any company seeking to profit from the digital realm. While Microsoft and TikTok-owner, ByteDance, have also joined the pursuit of a metaverse, [266] we'd be foolish to limit this problem to the biggest companies. While Big Tech is leading investment, the metaverse grows with each NFT, each purchase of cryptocurrency, each use of augmented reality through Snapchat and other platforms; justified through every DM, hashtag and upload, through the compulsive use of digital entertainment.

The metaverse has the potential to be worth $8 trillion in China alone. [267] Without the addition of small business, independent platforms and individual traders, this wouldn't be possible. Just as most businesses have a social media presence; baiting engagement through free coffee or a "shout-out", a presence in virtual reality will become normalised, with cryptocurrency and NFTs forming the basis of our economy.

Of course, we're not quite at *Ready Player One*; living in shacks and plugging into an "Oasis" of fully-immersed VR, complete with touch sensors. [268] But we're far enough.

In the future, the natural world can live on in digital form. No need to defend it. In our hubris, we even believe we can improve it. We edit our photos to make the stars brighter and – in VR – we can go even further; flying into space or swimming in imaginary seas.

And while there's currently no state-owned "digital space" (for example, a virtual reality park), it's only a matter of time until governments realise public space in VR is significantly cheaper than outdoor space. Just as physical infrastructure is more expensive than a smartphone (justifying chronic underinvestment in housing and communal space); we'll be funding VR parks and concert halls with our taxes, with the government promising they'll be "like nothing we've ever seen before. *A new frontier*."

-

In 1999, the Chili Peppers released *Californication*, a song about the superficiality of Hollywood and the culture it permeates throughout the United States. While this was no doubt prophetic, there is one line, in particular, that betrays the ignorance of the time: "Space may be the final frontier, but it's made in a Hollywood basement."[269] In just two decades, technology has regressed so far that the final frontier is no longer a physical place: it's a string of 1s and 0s. Today, the basement *is* the final frontier; powered by a server in the middle of the desert.

In the 90s, technology retained a singularity of purpose. Like the kid in the basement spending days playing video games, they were limited in scope; constrained by the boundaries of the platforms they used. Twenty years later, the Rubicon has finally been crossed: they're no longer playing games... they're living their lives.

Virtual reality is the logical extension of society-on-demand. It will mark the end: a final and complete exit from reality; of our physical existence and the world in which we live. The universe will be sacrificed at the altar of the metaverse: and we'll excuse it as essential.

Between the pandemic and cost of living crisis, against a backdrop of austerity and the decimation of public services, we have accelerated our drive into the End: and we're speeding downhill without brakes.

CONCLUSION

We're the middle children of history, man. No purpose or place. We have no Great War. No Great Depression. Our Great War's a spiritual war... our Great Depression is our lives. We've all been raised on television to believe that one day we'd all be millionaires, and movie gods, and rock stars. But we won't. And we're slowly learning that fact.

Tyler Durden, Fight Club.[270]

The social contract is dead.

Physical solidarity – in the presence of society-on-demand – is inherently weak, with hashtag activism forming the basis of social engagement.

We've moved from a society of strangers to a society which is, itself, estranged. Today, through the merging of digital and physical space, society has become a kind of mirage: we can see it, and yet – somehow – it remains inaccessible; where the space we physically occupy is different to the space we occupy in our minds: the phone in our pockets.

Society-on-demand becomes more systemic by the day, made not in Hollywood: but in Silicon Valley; backed by a compulsive digital entertainment industry, mainstream media and the highest levels of government.

MPs Tweet from their phones in the House of Commons, communicate via text in the tea rooms and bolster their position through legislation; supporting the industry at the public's expense.

In the 24 hour news cycle, gossip is information; entertainment is hope; ignorance is knowledge. We live our lives vicariously through the fiction of sensationalised media; where we idolise the lives of others, prioritising a vacuous existence at our own expense; an existence bereft of fulfilment, hope and peace.

The government is happy to oblige, not just through its own legitimisation of pornography and social media, but digital entertainment as a whole: the cinema in Downing Street, intervening in the Super League, MPs watching porn, the inadequate *Online Safety Bill*, scrapping the license fee, privatising Channel 4[271] and making the digital economy not just the fastest growing industry, but an industry essential to the economy at large; an economy based on smartphones, social media and digital entertainment; an acceleration of capitalism built on society-on-demand, fuelling the digitisation of physical space.

In the wake of several crises (with more to come), young people are facing a triple pandemic of mental illness, economic injustice and environmental catastrophe; with 1 in 6 children having a probable mental disorder in 2021; an increase from 1 in 9 in 2017.[272]

We need immediate solutions: and yet, immediate solutions are not forthcoming, with the government choosing to inflict further damage on a public too apathetic to resist.

The impact of smartphones, social media and pornography on mental health is disastrous; changing our perceptions, values and identity. We seek refuge in the oppression of these products, presented as our only solution to the problems we face in a calamitous cycle of cause and effect.

Against a backdrop of callous hearts, broken minds and shallow values, young people live in a society which is radically compromised, not just on a planetary scale, with climate change leading us towards mass extinction (not least the complete destruction of the environment with plants, animals, insects, oceans and seas facing catastrophic damage in a prolonged extinction event causing immense pain, suffering and abuse); but, additionally, a world in which relationships are defined as much by their interaction online as they are in person; debasing their humanity and, consequently, the ability to show meaningful solidarity; to physically organise for political change.

Our relationships are detached from physical space; our perceptions corrupted by the division and pressure these platforms impose: and we embrace it. Gen Z is the first generation to spend most of its childhood in the public eye, with every action and opinion recorded; with continuous surveillance leading to self-regulation, lack of development and hyper vigilance at the expense of mental health and personal growth, corrupting identity and breaking relationships.

We've sacrificed our entire character at the altar of Big Tech; driven by our desire for exposure and validation, allowing algorithms to form our identity, frame narratives and shape our interests through the prism of society-on-demand.

When the social fabric of society has been frayed this much, the tear is only going to get worse.

Our negation of physical existence will leave future generations without an alternative to the Online, with an increased lack of physical space, a depleted natural world and economic injustice fuelling their desire to not just retreat: but base their entire existence in the digital realm.

Under constant pressure to socialise, perform and be available online *and* succeed in school, work and at home, young people face a duality of pressures; with physical society and society-on-demand squeezing them from both sides.

In the past, we'd face challenges in person. Today, young people face challenges in person in addition to the ones they face online.

These parallel societies cannot coexist. When physical reality becomes the basis for the "more important" – "more preferable" – society-on-demand, the game is up.

Yet again, the government chooses to look the other way, presiding over social and planetary collapse.

The political solutions we need are cynically withheld; the knowledge that 24/7 surveillance and the compulsive nature of these products not only limits our action to the Online: but our actions actively damage the causes we're fighting for through the elevation of the political Right. Meanwhile, the establishment picks up the pieces of a broken society, benefitting from the safety of physical space – a space vacated by any semblance of meaningful opposition – while the Left campaigns via hashtag and glories in irrelevance.

And yet, the impotence we feel is a product of fiction, chained in the delusion of the products we use. We believe the smartphone, social media and direct messaging empower us yet, as we've seen, they radicalise and placate us, leaving us more impatient, less happy and less able to succeed.

When we reduce our engagement to the arena of social media, our action tends to follow the same location: online. For the Left, radicalisation meets impotence, a cocktail of futility, screaming into the void with the despair of inaction.

Society-on-demand has made cowardice our default characteristic, refusing the inconvenience and hardship of physical existence. The Tweet, the post, the like, the share, the comment, the DM: these are delusions, allowing us to avoid the necessity – the reality – of physical change.

Change is viewed as inevitable under the right conditions: but these conditions are now instrumental in its prevention through the impotence and apathy of the digital Present. Once again, it's young people who are most affected; spending their formative years in a deeply dysfunctional society, seeking refuge in society-on-demand.

-

The challenges we face cannot be defeated on an individual basis, nor overcome while the realm of the Online, through digital entertainment, is seen as preferable to the physical society in which we live. Expecting millions to demand change when apathy is god and escape is heaven is like trying to fit a camel through the lens of an iPhone.

And yet, when society continues to degrade, not only does political change become more urgent: it becomes more difficult.

The existing "tool" of social media is, clearly, not going to work. Instead, we need to free ourselves from the shackles of these systems, building new tools online and in person.

Fortunately, digital entertainment contains its own means of escape: "Delete Account."

We need to replace the fiction of empowerment through society-on-demand with the reality of empowerment through physical existence: an appreciation of our selves, each other and the natural world: a life beyond the smartphone.

For many of us, this doesn't exist. Gen Alpha doesn't know any different. Gen Z barely knows the difference. It's up to Millennials and Gen X – young enough to experience their own enslavement to these systems but old enough to remember life outside them – to fix this; demonstrating not just an existence away from society-on-demand, but to demonstrate its value.

This is the only way to begin. We cannot liberate ourselves in a prison of digital slavery; a prison run for and controlled by Big Tech and its allies. Instead, physical liberation can only occur outside the prisons we've checked ourselves into.

We need to establish platforms of meaningful information, strategy and analysis, uncorrupted by the algorithms of Big Tech and the burden of continuous engagement.

We need to treat the Online the same as society in person: limited by time and place. No dipping in and out; no incessant checks; no meaningless interaction: we need to consume with intention.

We need to prioritise information for physical action; a digital space to share physical meetings and protests. We cannot continue to leave this to Facebook's Events page or hashtags on other platforms. We need a calendar of accessible information; by cause, time, location and result; available to all, whether they're on social media or not, beyond the control of Big Tech.

In this way, the internet can empower and propel our actions offline, allowing us to build spaces of actual consequence, enabling physical solidarity through in person relationships and events.

What's Next?

The retreat of continuous, digital consumption is not just a dereliction of duty: it's woefully insufficient. Society-on-demand not only inflicts personal crises through mental illness and spiritual poverty: it also placates us from delivering the change we might otherwise achieve; blinding us through entertainment and meaningless content; personalising our problems while, at the same time, removing our agency to resolve them.

While the Left cites injustice as motivation for change, society-on-demand motivates apathy and, with it, the balance of power to ensure these motivations are destroyed.

Our rejection of physical reality has created a keyboard society, where the escape is seen as essential for radical change, to shift the debate and enter a space of political triumph: the option to control an alternative narrative, deleting the status quo.

And yet, when the retreat is portrayed as resistance, crashing the computer isn't enough: we need a system reboot.

We need to be brave: and that means facing up to our responsibilities, to the physical challenges we face, not just for our selves (although, that's certainly a good enough reason!), but for others; for those of us who, for whatever reason, are unable to do so.

Without the restoration of agency; without seeing clearly the augmented reality of our own lives and without our own mental wellbeing; we will continue our descent into society-on-demand; rejecting our dissent for the reality at hand.

Only when we resolve to retake our humanity – to tear it from the jaws of a destructive, divisive and pervasive digital entertainment industry – can we reclaim our lives; to overcome society-on-demand... and confront the demands on society.

REFERENCES

[1] Bowyer-Crane, C., Bonetti, S., Compton, S., Nielsen, D., D'apice, K. and Tracey, L. (2021). *The impact of Covid-19 on School Starters: Interim briefing 1 Parent and school concerns about children starting school.* [online] Available at: https://d2tic4wvo1iusb.cloudfront.net/documents/project s/Impact_of_Covid19_on_School_Starters_-_Interim_Briefing_1_-_April_2021_-_Final.pdf. (Accessed 15 February, 2022).

[2] Inc, L. (2017). *Gen Z and Millennials now more likely to communicate with each other digitally than in person.* [online] www.prnewswire.com. Available at: https://www.prnewswire.com/news-releases/gen-z-and-millennials-now-more-likely-to-communicate-with-each-other-digitally-than-in-person-300537770.html and https://liveperson.docsend.com/view/tm8j45m. (Accessed 15 February, 2022).

[3] YouGov. (n.d.). *Would Brits rather time-travel to the past or to the future?* [online] Available at: https://yougov.co.uk/topics/philosophy/trackers/would-brits-rather-time-travel-to-the-past-or-to-the-future?crossBreak=1824. (Accessed 15 February, 2022).

[4] Sehmi, R. and Slaughter, H. (2021). *Double trouble Exploring the labour market and mental health impact of Covid-19 on young people.* [online] Resolution Foundation. Quoted from "Key findings" summary available at: https://www.resolutionfoundation.org/publications/doubl e-trouble. (Accessed 15 February, 2022).

[5] Ibid.

[6] Ofcom (2021). *Media Nations: UK 2021.* [online] Ofcom. Available at: https://www.ofcom.org.uk/__data/assets/pdf_file/0023/222890/media-nations-report-2021.pdf. (Accessed 15 February, 2022).

[7] Ofcom (2020). *Lockdown leads to surge in TV screen time and streaming.* [online] Ofcom. Available at: https://www.ofcom.org.uk/about-ofcom/latest/media/media-releases/2020/lockdown-leads-to-surge-in-tv-screen-time-and-streaming. (Accessed 15 February, 2022)

[8] Department for Digital, Culture, Media and Sport (2020). *DCMS Sectors Economic Estimates 2018 (provisional): Gross Value Added.* [online] DCMS. Available at: https://assets.publishing.service.gov.uk/government/uploads/system/uploads/attachment_data/file/959053/DCMS_Sectors_Economic_Estimates_GVA_2018_V2.pdf. (Accessed 15 February, 2022)

[9] ukactive (2018). *UK adults spend 12 hours a week watching on-demand TV but only 90 minutes exercising.* [online] ukactive. Available at: https://www.ukactive.com/news/uk-adults-spend-12-hours-a-week-watching-on-demand-tv-but-only-90-minutes-exercising. (Accessed 15 February, 2022)

[10] PwC (2021). *UK edition: Entertainment & Media Outlook 2021-2025.* [online] PwC. Available at: https://www.pwc.co.uk/industries/technology-media-and-telecommunications/insights/entertainment-media-outlook.html. (Accessed 15 February, 2022)

[11] Ofcom (2021). *Children and parents: media use and attitudes report.* [online] Ofcom. Available at: https://www.ofcom.org.uk/__data/assets/pdf_file/0025/217825/children-and-parents-media-use-and-attitudes-report-2020-21.pdf. (Accessed 15 February, 2022)

[12] Ibid.

[13] Ibid.

[14] Girlguiding (2020). *Girlguiding research briefing: Early findings on the impact of Covid-19 on girls and young women.* [online] Girlguiding. Available at: https://www.girlguiding.org.uk/globalassets/docs-and-resources/research-and-campaigns/girlguiding-covid19-research-briefing.pdf. (Accessed 15 February, 2022).

[15] YGAM. (2021). *BLOG: Is Squid Game an opportunity to have safeguarding conversations with young Netflix viewers?* [online] YGAM. Available at: https://www.ygam.org/blog-is-squid-game-an-opportunity-to-have-safeguarding-conversations-with-young-netflix-viewers. (Accessed 15 February, 2022).

[16] Milmo, Dan. (2021). *TechScape: what to expect from the online safety bill.* [online] The Guardian. Available at: https://www.theguardian.com/technology/2021/nov/10/techscape-online-safety-bill-ofcom. (Accessed 15 February, 2022).

[17] Heffer, Greg. (2021). *Boris Johnson and staff use £2.6m White House-style briefing room in Downing Street to watch new James Bond film.* [online] Sky News. Available at: https://news.sky.com/story/boris-johnson-and-staff-use-2-6m-white-house-style-briefing-room-in-downing-street-to-watch-new-james-bond-film-12441531. (Accessed 15 February, 2022).

[18] Thoreau, David Henry. (1854). *Walden.* [Book] Ticknor and Fields.

[19] *Carousel of Progress.* (1994). [Theme Park Attraction] Walt Disney World.

[20] *Jurassic Park.* (1993). [Motion Picture] Universal Pictures.

[21] The Good Place. Season 4. (2020). *Whenever You're Ready.* [TV Show] Netflix.

[22] Wakefield, Jane. (2022). *How will Tonga's broken internet cable be mended?* [online] BBC News. Available at: https://www.bbc.co.uk/news/technology-60069066. (Accessed 15 February, 2022).

[23] NEC. (n.d.). *Submarine Cable Systems: Products & Solutions.* [online] NEC. Available at: https://www.nec.com/en/global/prod/nw/submarine. (Accessed 15 February, 2022).

[24] Arthur, Charles. (2013). *Undersea internet cables off Egypt disrupted as navy arrests three.* [online] The Guardian. Available at: https://www.theguardian.com/technology/2013/mar/28/

egypt-undersea-cable-arrests. (Accessed 15 February, 2022).

25 Johnson, Bobbie. (2008). *Internet connection cut between Europe, Asia and Africa.* [online] The Guardian. Available at: https://www.theguardian.com/world/2008/dec/21/internet-cable-cut. (Accessed 15 February, 2022).

26 Wakefield, Jane. (2022). *How will Tonga's broken internet cable be mended?* [online] BBC News. Available at: https://www.bbc.co.uk/news/technology-60069066. (Accessed 15 February, 2022).

27 TeleGeography (n.d.). *Submarine Cable FAQs.* [online] TeleGeography. Available at: https://www2.telegeography.com/submarine-cable-faqs-frequently-asked-questions. (Accessed 15 February, 2022).

28 Genius. (2007). *Steve Jobs – IPhone Keynote 2007.* [online] Genius. Available at: https://genius.com/Steve-jobs-iphone-keynote-2007-annotated. (Accessed 15 February, 2022).

29 Ibid.

30 Apple Newsroom. (2007). *Apple Reinvents the Phone with iPhone.* [online] Apple. Available at: https://www.apple.com/newsroom/2007/01/09Apple-Reinvents-the-Phone-with-iPhone. (Accessed 15 February, 2022).

31 Ibid.

32 Genius. (2007). *Steve Jobs – IPhone Keynote 2007.* [online] Genius. Available at: https://genius.com/Steve-jobs-iphone-keynote-2007-annotated. (Accessed 15 February, 2022).

33 Andrew, Scottie. (2020). *The FBI has opened an investigation into the shooting death of Kentucky EMT Breonna Taylor.* [online] CNN, S.A. Available at: https://edition.cnn.com/2020/05/21/us/breonna-taylor-death-police-changes-trnd/index.html. (Accessed 15 February, 2022).

34 Hu, Y. and Qian, Y. (2021). COVID-19, Inter-household Contact and Mental Well-Being Among Older Adults in the

US and the UK. *Frontiers in Sociology, (6).* [online] Frontiers in Sociology. Available at: https://www.frontiersin.org/article/10.3389/fsoc.2021.71 4626. (Accessed 15 February, 2022).

35 yougov.co.uk. (2018). *YouGov reveals the extent of Britain's addiction to our phones | YouGov.* [online] YouGov. Available at: https://yougov.co.uk/topics/technology/articles-reports/2018/10/18/yougov-reveals-extent-britains-addiction-our-phone. (Accessed 15 February, 2022).

36 Youngs, Ian. (2021). *Young viewers prefer TV subtitles, research suggests.* [online] BBC News. Available at: https://www.bbc.co.uk/news/entertainment-arts-59259964. (Accessed 15 February, 2022).

37 Ofcom. (2016). *The UK is now a smartphone society.* [online] Ofcom. Available at: https://www.ofcom.org.uk/about-ofcom/latest/media/media-releases/2015/cmr-uk-2015. (Accessed 15 February, 2022).

38 yougov.co.uk. (2018). *YouGov reveals the extent of Britain's addiction to our phones | YouGov.* [online] YouGov. Available at: https://yougov.co.uk/topics/technology/articles-reports/2018/10/18/yougov-reveals-extent-britains-addiction-our-phone. (Accessed 15 February, 2022).

39 IMDbPro. (2019). *Top Lifetime Grosses - Box Office Mojo.* [online] Box Office Mojo. Available at: https://www.boxofficemojo.com/chart/top_lifetime_gros s/?area=XWW. (Accessed 15 February, 2022).

40 Game of Thrones. Season 8. (2018). *The Iron Throne.* [TV Show] HBO.

41 Sohn Sei Yon, Krasnoff Lauren, Rees Philippa, Kalk Nicola J., Carter Ben. (2021). The Association Between Smartphone Addiction and Sleep: A UK Cross-Sectional Study of Young Adults. *Frontiers in Psychiatry, (12).* [online] Frontiers in Psychiatry. Available at: https://www.frontiersin.org/article/10.3389/fpsyt.2021.6 29407. (Accessed 15 February, 2022).

42 NHS Digital (2021). *Mental Health of Children and Young People in England, 2021 Wave 2 follow up to the 2017 survey.* [online] NHS Digital. Available at: https://files.digital.nhs.uk/97/B09EF8/mhcyp_2021_rep.pdf. (Accessed 15 February, 2022).

43 YouGov. (2018). *YouGov reveals the extent of Britain's addiction to our phones | YouGov.* [online] YouGov. Available at: https://yougov.co.uk/topics/technology/articles-reports/2018/10/18/yougov-reveals-extent-britains-addiction-our-phone. (Accessed 15 February, 2022).

44 BARB. (2021). *Four-screen viewing now includes smartphone data | BARB.* [online] BARB. Available at: https://www.barb.co.uk/news/dovetail-fusion-now-includes-smartphone-data. (Accessed 15 February, 2022).

45 Davis, N. (2019). *One in four children "have problematic smartphone use."* [online] The Guardian. Available at: https://www.theguardian.com/society/2019/nov/29/one-in-four-children-have-problematic-smartphone-use. (Accessed 15 February, 2022).

46 YouGov. (2018). *YouGov reveals the extent of Britain's addiction to our phones | YouGov.* [online] YouGov. Available at: https://yougov.co.uk/topics/technology/articles-reports/2018/10/18/yougov-reveals-extent-britains-addiction-our-phone. (Accessed 15 February, 2022).

47 Viner, Russell. Davie, Max. Firth, Alison. *The health impacts of screen time: a guide for clinicians and parents Contents.* (2019). [online] RCPCH. Available at: https://www.rcpch.ac.uk/sites/default/files/2018-12/rcpch_screen_time_guide_-_final.pdf. (Accessed 15 February, 2022).

48 Clark, C. and Picton, I. (2021). *Children and young people's reading engagement in 2021 Emerging insight into the impact of the Covid-19 pandemic on reading.* [online] Literacy Trust. Available at:

https://cdn.literacytrust.org.uk/media/documents/Readin g_in_2021.pdf. (Accessed 15 February, 2022).
⁴⁹ Ibid.
⁵⁰ Ibid.
⁵¹ Ofcom. (2020). *Ofcom Children's Media Lives Life in Lockdown.* [online] Ofcom. Available at:
https://www.ofcom.org.uk/__data/assets/pdf_file/0024/ 200976/cml-life-in-lockdown-report.pdf. (Accessed 15 February, 2022).
⁵² Ibid.
⁵³ Small, G. W., Lee, J., Kaufman, A., Jalil, J., Siddarth, P., Gaddipati, H., Moody, T. D., & Bookheimer, S. Y. (2020). Brain health consequences of digital technology use. *Dialogues in Clinical Neuroscience*, *22*(2), 179–187. [Online] PubMed.Gov. Available at:
https://doi.org/10.31887/DCNS.2020.22.2/gsmall. (Accessed 15 February, 2022).
⁵⁴ Firth, J., Torous, J., Stubbs, B., Firth, J. A., Steiner, G. Z., Smith, L., Alvarez-Jimenez, M., Gleeson, J., Vancampfort, D., Armitage, C. J., & Sarris, J. (2019). The "online brain": how the Internet may be changing our cognition. *World Psychiatry: Official Journal of the World Psychiatric Association (WPA)*, *18*(2), 119–129. [Online] Wiley Online Library. Available at:
https://doi.org/10.1002/wps.20617. (Accessed 15 February, 2022).
⁵⁵ Peng, M., Chen, X., Zhao, Q., & Zhou, Z. (2018). Attentional scope is reduced by Internet use: A behavior and ERP study. *PLOS One*, *13*(6), e0198543. [Online] PloS One. Available at:
https://doi.org/10.1371/journal.pone.0198543. (Accessed 15 February, 2022).
⁵⁶ Crestodina, A. (2019). *[New Research] How has Blogging Changed? 5 Years of Blogging Statistics, Data and Trends.* [online] Orbit Media Studios. Available at:
https://www.orbitmedia.com/blog/blogging-statistics. (Accessed 15 February, 2022).

57 O'Neill-Hart, Celie. (2017). *Self-directed learning from YouTube.* [online] Think With Google. Available at: https://www.thinkwithgoogle.com/marketing-strategies/video/self-directed-learning-youtube. (Accessed 15 February, 2022).

58 Matney, L. (2017). *YouTube has 1.5 billion logged-in monthly users watching a ton of mobile video.* [online] TechCrunch. Available at: https://techcrunch.com/2017/06/22/youtube-has-1-5-billion-logged-in-monthly-users-watching-a-ton-of-mobile-video. (Accessed 15 February, 2022).

59 Wiers, Ashley. (2020). *How people use YouTube to learn at home.* [online] Think With Google. Available at: https://www.thinkwithgoogle.com/consumer-insights/consumer-trends/how-people-use-youtube-for-learning. (Accessed 15 February, 2022).

60 Jones, P. (2018). *Beyond Millennials: The Next Generation of Learners.* [online] Pearson. Available at: https://www.pearson.com/content/dam/one-dot-com/one-dot-com/global/Files/news/news-annoucements/2018/The-Next-Generation-of-Learners_final.pdf. (Accessed 15 February, 2022).

61 Poynter. (2022). *An open letter to YouTube's CEO from the world's fact-checkers.* [online] Poynter. Available at: https://www.poynter.org/fact-checking/2022/an-open-letter-to-youtubes-ceo-from-the-worlds-fact-checkers. (Accessed 15 February, 2022).

62 Solsman, J.E. (2018). *Ever get caught in an unexpected hourlong YouTube binge? Thank YouTube AI for that.* [online] CNET. Available at: https://www.cnet.com/tech/services-and-software/youtube-ces-2018-neal-mohan. (Accessed 15 February, 2022).

63 Poynter. (2022). *An open letter to YouTube's CEO from the world's fact-checkers.* [online] Poynter. Available at: https://www.poynter.org/fact-checking/2022/an-open-letter-to-youtubes-ceo-from-the-worlds-fact-checkers. (Accessed 15 February, 2022).

64 National Literacy Trust. (2019). *Children, young people and digital reading*. [online] National Literacy Trust. Available at: https://literacytrust.org.uk/research-services/research-reports/children-young-people-and-digital-reading. (Accessed 15 February, 2022).

65 Hinsliff, Gabby. (2022). *"My son cowers when a shopkeeper says hello" – are the toddlers of Covid all right?* [online] The Guardian. Available at: https://www.theguardian.com/world/2022/jan/29/my-son-cowers-when-a-shopkeeper-says-hello-are-the-toddlers-of-covid-all-right. (Accessed 15 February, 2022).

66 BBC News. (2022). *"Levelling up" plan for UK unveiled by Michael Gove*. [online] BBC News. Available at: https://www.bbc.co.uk/news/uk-politics-60216307. (Accessed 15 February, 2022).

67 Beland, L.-P. and Murphy, R. Centre for Economic Performance, LSE. (2015). *Ill Communication: Technology, Distraction & Student Performance*. [online] LSE. Available at: https://cep.lse.ac.uk/pubs/download/dp1350.pdf. (Accessed 15 February, 2022).

68 Mancall-Bitel, N. (2019). *How can a distracted generation learn anything?* [online] BBC. Available at: https://www.bbc.com/worklife/article/20190220-how-can-a-distracted-generation-learn-anything. (Accessed 15 February, 2022).

69 Josephs, Jonathan. (2022). *US airlines warn of impending 5G flight disruption*. [online] BBC News. Available at: https://www.bbc.co.uk/news/business-60036831. (Accessed 15 February, 2022).

70 Calder, Simon. (2022). *All the flights that have been cancelled due to 5G rollout*. [online] The Independent. Available at: https://www.independent.co.uk/travel/news-and-advice/5g-flights-cancelled-british-airways-emirates-b1996023.html. (Accessed 15 February, 2022).

71 Wattles, J., Muntean, P., Wallace, G. (2022). *The 5G-airline snafu: Everything we know*. [online] CNN. Available at:

https://edition.cnn.com/2022/01/19/tech/airlines-5g-flights-canceled-explainer/index.html. (Accessed 3 May, 2022).

72 Reality Check Team. (2019). *Are these masts dangerous or is it just fearmongering?* [online] BBC News. Available at: https://www.bbc.co.uk/news/world-europe-48616174. (Accessed 15 February, 2022).

73 Ofcom. (2016). *The UK is now a smartphone society.* [online] Ofcom. Available at: https://www.ofcom.org.uk/about-ofcom/latest/media/media-releases/2015/cmr-uk-2015. (Accessed 15 February, 2022).

74 Ofcom. (2013). *Infrastructure Report.* [online] Ofcom. Available at: https://www.ofcom.org.uk/__data/assets/pdf_file/0027/58644/iru_2013.pdf. (Accessed 15 February, 2022).

75 Adams, Richard. (2017). *Hundreds of children's playgrounds in England close due to cuts.* [online] The Guardian. Available at: https://www.theguardian.com/uk-news/2017/apr/13/hundreds-of-childrens-playgrounds-in-england-close-owing-to-cuts. (Accessed 15 February, 2022).

76 RCPCH. *What do children and young people think about screen time?* (2019). [online] RCPCH. Available at: https://www.rcpch.ac.uk/sites/default/files/2018-12/rcpch_screen_time_full_cyp_views.pdf. (Accessed 15 February, 2022).

77 Moss, S. (2012). *Natural Childhood.* [online] National Trust. Available at: https://nt.global.ssl.fastly.net/documents/read-our-natural-childhood-report.pdf. (Accessed 15 February, 2022).

78 Pyle, R. (2003) 'Nature Matrix: reconnecting people and nature'. Oryx 37(2): 206–214. Accessed via: Moss, S. (2012). *Natural Childhood.* [online] National Trust. Available at: https://nt.global.ssl.fastly.net/documents/read-our-

natural-childhood-report.pdf. (Accessed 15 February, 2022).

[79] Louv, R. (2005) Last Child in the Woods: Saving Our Children from Nature-Deficit Disorder, Algonquin Books, Chapel Hill, p.34. Accessed via: Moss, S. (2012). *Natural Childhood.* [online] National Trust. Available at: https://nt.global.ssl.fastly.net/documents/read-our-natural-childhood-report.pdf. (Accessed 15 February, 2022).

[80] Gaster, S. (1991) 'Urban Children's Access to Their Neighbourhoods: Changes
Over Three Generations', quoted in Louv, R. (2005) Last Child in the Woods, p.123. Accessed via: Moss, S. (2012). *Natural Childhood.* [online] National Trust. Available at: https://nt.global.ssl.fastly.net/documents/read-our-natural-childhood-report.pdf. (Accessed 15 February, 2022).

[81] Ofcom. (2021). *Online Nation 2021 Report.* [online] Ofcom. Available at: https://www.ofcom.org.uk/__data/assets/pdf_file/0013/220414/online-nation-2021-report.pdf. (Accessed 15 February, 2022).

[82] LivePerson, Inc. (2017). *Gen Z and Millennials now more likely to communicate with each other digitally than in person.* [online] PR Newswire. Available at: https://www.prnewswire.com/news-releases/gen-z-and-millennials-now-more-likely-to-communicate-with-each-other-digitally-than-in-person-300537770.html. (Accessed 15 February, 2022).

[83] Hume, Robert. (2020). *Slaves to the rhythm: 100 years of the robot.* [online] Irish Examiner. Available at: https://www.irishexaminer.com/lifestyle/artsandculture/arid-40046318.html. (Accessed 15 February, 2022).

[84] Freeman, M.J. (n.d.). *Verbally interactive telephone interrogation system with selectible variable decision tree.* Patent filed by Michael J. Freeman (1979). [online] Available at:

https://patents.google.com/patent/US4320256. (Accessed 15 February, 2022).

85 Akhtar, Allana and Ward, Marguerite. (2018). *Bill Gates and Steve Jobs raised their kids tech-free — and it should've been a red flag.* [online] Business Insider. Available at: https://www.businessinsider.com/screen-time-limits-bill-gates-steve-jobs-red-flag-2017-10. (Accessed 15 February, 2022).

86 Fox News. (2019). *Mark Zuckerberg weighs in on the good and bad of social media.* [online] Fox News. Available at: https://video.foxnews.com/v/6095989196001#sp=show-clips. (Accessed 15 February, 2022).

87 Zubrow, Keith. Gavrilovic, Maria. Ortiz, Alex. (2021). *Whistleblower's SEC complaint: Facebook knew platform was used to "promote human trafficking and domestic servitude."* [online] CBS News. Available at: https://www.cbsnews.com/news/facebook-whistleblower-sec-complaint-60-minutes-2021-10-04. (Accessed 15 February, 2022).

88 Auxier, B. and Anderson, M. (2021). *Social Media Use in 2021.* [online] Pew Research Center. Available at: https://www.pewresearch.org/internet/2021/04/07/social-media-use-in-2021. (Accessed 15 February, 2022).

89 Allen, M. (2017). *Sean Parker unloads on Facebook: "God only knows what it's doing to our children's brains."* [online] Axios. Available at: https://www.axios.com/sean-parker-unloads-on-facebook-2508036343.html. (Accessed 15 February, 2022).

90 Ibid.

91 Stanford Graduate School of Business. (2017). *Chamath Palihapitiya, Founder and CEO Social Capital, on Money as an Instrument of Change.* [online] YouTube. Available at: https://www.youtube.com/watch?v=PMotykw0SIk&t=1281s. (Accessed 15 February, 2022).

92 Cooper, A. (2017). *What is "brain hacking"? Tech insiders on why you should care.* [online] CBS News.

Available at: https://www.cbsnews.com/news/brain-hacking-tech-insiders-60-minutes. (Accessed 15 February, 2022).

93 Ibid.

94 Ibid.

95 CBS News. (2022). *Trump's new app, "Truth Social," begins slow rollout.* [online] CBS News. Available at: https://www.cbsnews.com/news/trumps-new-app-truth-social-slow-rollout. (Accessed 21 Ferbruary,. 2022).

96 Curb Your Enthusiasm. Season 10. (2020). [TV Show]. HBO.

97 Thompson, Alex. (2020). *Why the right wing has a massive advantage on Facebook.* [online] Politico. Available at: https://www.politico.com/news/2020/09/26/facebook-conservatives-2020-421146. (Accessed 15 February, 2020).

98 Zubrow, Keith. Gavrilovic, Maria. Ortiz, Alex. (2021). *Whistleblower's SEC complaint: Facebook knew platform was used to "promote human trafficking and domestic servitude."* [online] CBS News. Available at: https://www.cbsnews.com/news/facebook-whistleblower-sec-complaint-60-minutes-2021-10-04. (Accessed 15 February, 2022).

99 Haugen, Francis (4th October, 2021). United States Senate Committee on Commerce, Science and Transportation. Sub-Committee on Consumer Protection, Product Safety, and Data Security. [online]. Available at: https://www.commerce.senate.gov/services/files/FC8A55 8E-824E-4914-BEDB-3A7B1190BD49. (Accessed 15 February, 2022).

100 Huszár, F., Ktena, S.I., O'Brien, C., Belli, L., Schlaikjer, A. and Hardt, M. (2021). *Algorithmic amplification of politics on Twitter.* Proceedings of the National Academy of Sciences, 119(1), p.e2025334119. [online] Twitter. Available at: https://cdn.cms-twdigitalassets.com/content/dam/blog-twitter/official/en_us/company/2021/rml/Algorithmic-

Amplification-of-Politics-on-Twitter.pdf. (Accessed 15 February, 2022).

[101] Jones, Owen. (2022). *The Met: A National Disgrace.* [online] YouTube. Available at: https://www.youtube.com/watch?v=A-XbdruSmw0. (Accessed 15 February, 2022).

[102] BBC News. (2022). *Rayan: Moroccan boy trapped in well for four days dies.* [online] BBC News. Available at: https://www.bbc.co.uk/news/world-africa-60275177. (Accessed 15 February, 2022).

[103] KTRK (2021). *Baby Jessica fell down a well on Oct. 14, 1987.* [online] ABC13 Houston. Available at: https://abc13.com/baby-jessica-rescuing-saving-from-well-mcclure/5620354. (Accessed 15 February, 2022)

[104] Gavilan, Jodesz. (2016). *Duterte's P10M social media campaign: Organic, volunteer-driven.* [online] Rappler. Available at: https://www.rappler.com/newsbreak/134979-rodrigo-duterte-social-media-campaign-nic-gabunada. (Accessed 15 February, 2022).

[105] Auchard, E and Ingram, D. (2018). *Cambridge Analytica CEO claims influence on U.S. election, Facebook questioned.* [online] Reuters. Available at: https://www.reuters.com/article/us-facebook-cambridge-analytica-idUSKBN1GW1SG. (Accessed 15 February, 2022).

[106] Ofcom. (2021). *Online Nation 2021 Report.* [online] Ofcom. Available at: https://www.ofcom.org.uk/__data/assets/pdf_file/0013/220414/online-nation-2021-report.pdf. (Accessed 15 February, 2022).

[107] Moya Lothian-McLean (2019). *How do your porn habits compare with young people across Britain?* [online] BBC Three. Available at: https://www.bbc.co.uk/bbcthree/article/bb79a2ce-0de4-4965-98f0-9ebbcfcc2a60. (Accessed 15 February, 2022).

[108] BBC Bitesize. (n.d.). *The use of public capital punishment up to the 19th century - Methods of*

punishment – WJEC - GCSE History Revision - WJEC. [online] BBC Bitesize. Available at: https://www.bbc.co.uk/bitesize/guides/z938v9q/revision/2. (Accessed 15 February, 2022).
[109] BBC Bitesize. (n.d.). *The use of public capital punishment up to the 19th century - Methods of punishment – WJEC - GCSE History Revision - WJEC.* [online] BBC Bitesize. Available at: https://www.bbc.co.uk/bitesize/guides/z938v9q/revision/3. (Accessed 15 February, 2022).
[110] Knowles, J. (2015). *The Abolition of the Death Penalty in the United Kingdom How it Happened and Why it Still Matters.* [online] Death Penalty Project. Available at: https://www.deathpenaltyproject.org/wp-content/uploads/2017/12/DPP-50-Years-on-pp1-68-1.pdf. (Accessed 15 February, 2022).
[111] Ibid.
[112] Evans, Jamie and Cross, Katie. (2021). *The Geography of Gambling Premises in Britain.* [online] Financial Fairness. Available at: https://www.financialfairness.org.uk/docs?editionId=c8d6f9b5-1c8b-4b97-9bb4-c3099938f737. (Accessed 15 February, 2022).
[113] Smith, Matthew. (2018). *Here's what Britain's ideal high street looks like | YouGov.* [online] YouGov. Available at: https://yougov.co.uk/topics/consumer/articles-reports/2018/06/29/heres-what-britains-ideal-high-street-looks. (Accessed 15 February, 2022).
[114] Gambling Commission. (2021). *Statistics on participation and problem gambling for the year to September 2021.* [online] Gambling Commission. Available at: https://www.gamblingcommission.gov.uk/statistics-and-research/publication/statistics-on-participation-and-problem-gambling-for-the-year-to-september. (Accessed 15 February, 2022).
[115] Department for Digital, Culture, Media and Sport (2020). *DCMS Sectors Economic Estimates 2018*

(provisional): Gross Value Added. [online] DCMS. Available at: https://assets.publishing.service.gov.uk/government/uploads/system/uploads/attachment_data/file/959053/DCMS_Sectors_Economic_Estimates_GVA_2018_V2.pdf. (Accessed 15 February, 2022)

[116] O'Bryan, Joan. (2018). [online] *CIPFA Statistics and the Future of England's Libraries.* [Online] DCMS. Available at: https://assets.publishing.service.gov.uk/government/uploads/system/uploads/attachment_data/file/734348/Analysing_data-CIPFA_statistics.pdf. (Accessed 15 February, 2022).

[117] Gambling Commission. (2020). *Industry Statistics - November 2020.* [online] Gambling Commission. Available at: https://www.gamblingcommission.gov.uk/statistics-and-research/publication/industry-statistics-november-2020#key-facts. (Accessed 15 February, 2022).

[118] Cipfastats.net. (2018). *Spend on British libraries drops by nearly £20m.* [online] CIPFA Stats. Available at: https://www.cipfastats.net/news/newsstory.asp?content=23214. (Accessed 15 February, 2022).

[119] Perry, S.L. and Schleifer, C. (2017). *Till Porn Do Us Part? A Longitudinal Examination of Pornography Use and Divorce.* The Journal of Sex Research, 55(3), pp.284–296. [online]. Enough. Available at: https://www.enough.org/objects/Till_Porn_Do_Us_Part_A_Longitudinal_Exam_fnv.pdf. (Accessed 15 February, 2022).

[120] Sullivan, Margaret. (2021). *By bearing witness — and hitting "record" — 17-year-old Darnella Frazier may have changed the world.* [online] Washington Post. Available at: https://www.washingtonpost.com/lifestyle/media/darnella-frazier-george-floyd-trial/2021/04/20/9e261cc6-a1e2-11eb-a774-7b47ceb36ee8_story.html. (Accessed 15 February, 2022).

[121] Bona, E. (2015). *Bill Shankly remembered: 11 brilliant quotes from Liverpool's iconic manager.* [online] Liverpool Echo. Available at: https://www.liverpoolecho.co.uk/news/liverpool-news/bill-shankly-remembered-11-brilliant-10156199. (Accessed 15 February, 2022).

[122] Neville, Gary. (2021). *Gary Neville on European Super League plans: "I'm fuming... but it wont go through, not a chance."* [online] Sky Sports. Available at: https://www.skysports.com/football/news/11661/1227999 6/gary-neville-on-european-super-league-plans-im-fuming-but-it-wont-go-through-not-a-chance. (Accessed 15 February, 2022).

[123] Ibbetson, C. (2021). *Snap poll: football fans overwhelmingly reject European Super League | YouGov.* [online] YouGov. Available at: https://yougov.co.uk/topics/sport/articles-reports/2021/04/19/snap-poll-football-fans-overwhelmingly-reject-euro. (Accessed 15 February, 2022).

[124] Walker, Peter. (2021). *Government pledges to stop English clubs joining European Super League.* [online] The Guardian. Available at: https://www.theguardian.com/football/2021/apr/19/gove rnment-pledges-to-stop-english-clubs-joining-european-super-league. (Accessed 15 February, 2022).

[125] Ingle, Sean. (2021). *European Super League: government, FA and Uefa unite to denounce plans.* [online] The Guardian. Available at: https://www.theguardian.com/football/2021/apr/19/euro pean-super-league-government-fa-and-uefa-unite-to-denounce-plans. (Accessed 15 February, 2022).

[126] Footy. (n.d.). *Footballers vs Fans - Compare your wage with footballers'!* [online] Footy. Available at: https://www.footy.com/footballers-vs-the-fans/#premier-league. (Accessed 15 February, 2022).

[127] Premier League. (n.d.). *A record-breaking season.* [online] Premier League. Available at:

https://www.premierleague.com/season-review/the-fans/2164581?articleId=2164581. (Accessed 15 February, 2022).

128 Gazapo, Carlos. (n.d.). *Football TV Rights- The European Media Landscape. EPL Analysis.* [online] Sports Business Institute Barcelona. Available at: https://www.sbibarcelona.com/newsdetails/index/403. (Accessed 15 February, 2022).

129 Ernst & Young Global Limited (2022). *Premier League Economic and Social Impact.* [online] Premier League. Available at: https://resources.premierleague.com/premierleague/document/2022/01/17/b61d9bb0-1488-4cd1-be25-82be98073252/EYUK-000142222_PL-economic-and-social-contribution_28_Spread_HR_2.pdf. (Accessed 15 Feb. 2022).

130 Change. (n.d.). *Sign the Petition.* [online] Change. Available at: https://www.change.org/p/make-transfer-deadline-day-a-uk-national-holiday. (Accessed 16 February, 2022).

131 ONS. (2018). *Consumer trends, UK - Office for National Statistics.* [online] ONS. Available at: https://www.ons.gov.uk/economy/nationalaccounts/satelliteaccounts/bulletins/consumertrends/octobertodecember2018. (Accessed 16 February, 2022).

132 Alcohol Concern. (n.d.). *Alcohol and football.* [online] IAS. Available at: https://www.ias.org.uk/uploads/pdf/Marketing/Alcohol%20and%20Football_Briefing.pdf. (Accessed 16 February, 2022).

133 Slater, Matt. (2018). *Football's relationship with gambling "disturbing" and "worrying" warn experts.* [online] The Independent. Available at: https://www.independent.co.uk/sport/football/premier-league/football-betting-premier-league-epl-football-league-efl-sponsors-kits-201819-a8470936.html. (Accessed 16 February, 2022).

134 Press Association. (2018). *Number of clubs sponsored by betting firms is "disturbing", say campaigners.* [online] The Guardian. Available at: https://www.theguardian.com/football/2018/jul/30/campaigners-concerned-championship-efl-clubs-sponsored-betting. (Accessed 16 February, 2022).

135 Gambling Commission. (2021). *Statistics on participation and problem gambling for the year to September 2021.* [online] Gambling Commission. Available at: https://www.gamblingcommission.gov.uk/statistics-and-research/publication/statistics-on-participation-and-problem-gambling-for-the-year-to-september. (Accessed 16 February, 2022).

136 Duncan, P., Davies, R. and Sweney, M. (2018). *Children "bombarded" with betting adverts during World Cup.* [online] The Guardian. Available at: https://www.theguardian.com/media/2018/jul/15/children-bombarded-with-betting-adverts-during-world-cup. (Accessed 15 February, 2022).

137 YGAM. (2022). *New survey shows students use borrowed money to gamble.* [online] YGAM. Available at: https://www.ygam.org/new-survey-shows-students-use-borrowed-money-to-gamble. (Accessed 16 February, 2022).

138 Super 6. (n.d.). *Super 6 | Home.* [online] Sky Sports Super 6. Available at: https://super6.skysports.com. (Accessed 16 February, 2022).

139 BBC News. (2022). *Study finds avid fantasy football fans face mental health risk.* [online] BBC News. Available at: https://www.bbc.co.uk/news/uk-england-nottinghamshire-59881432?at_medium=RSS&at_campaign=KARANGA. (Accessed 16 February, 2022).

140 Pandey, Manish. (2022). *Just Stop Oil: Why protesters are tying themselves to goalposts.* [online] BBC News. Available at: https://www.bbc.co.uk/news/newsbeat-60795041. (Accessed 18 April, 2022).

141 Premier League. (2020). *Players' statement on Black Lives Matter.* [Online] Premier League. Available at: https://www.premierleague.com/news/1680826?sf23500 4418=1#. (Accessed 23 April, 2022).

142 BBC News. (2022). *Child Q: Strip-search Met officers put on desk duties last week.* [Online] BBC News. Available at: https://www.bbc.co.uk/news/uk-england-london-60858196. (Accessed 23 April, 2022).

143 Venables, Rachael. (2022). *Revealed: Most children strip-searched by Met come from ethnic backgrounds.* [online] LBC. Available at: https://www.lbc.co.uk/news/three-quarters-of-all-children-strip-searched-by-met-come-from-ethnically-divers/. (Accessed 23 April, 2022).

144 Home Office (2021). *The Police, Crime, Sentencing and Courts Bill.* [online] UK Government. Available at: https://www.gov.uk/government/collections/the-police-crime-sentencing-and-courts-bill. (Accessed 16 February, 2022).

145 Ibid.

146 George, C. (n.d.). *The ancient origins of the new nomads.* [online] BBC. Available at: https://www.bbc.com/culture/article/20210730-the-ancient-origins-of-the-new-nomads. (Accessed 16 February, 2022).

147 Hampton Institute. (n.d.). *"It's A Class Struggle, Goddammit!": A Speech by Fred Hampton (1969).* [online] Hampton Think. Available at: https://www.hamptonthink.org/read/its-a-class-struggle-goddammit-fred-hampton. (Accessed 16 February, 2022).

148 Tighe, Siobhann. (2017). *Is it OK to watch porn in public?* [online] BBC News. Available at: https://www.bbc.co.uk/news/magazine-38611265. (Accessed 16 February, 2022).

149 Ibid.

150 BBC News. (2017). *Planes, trains and McDonald's: Your stories of porn in public.* [online] BBC News.

Available at: https://www.bbc.co.uk/news/magazine-38638339. (Accessed 16 February, 2022).

[151] Ibid.

[152] Grant, Harriet. (2021). *"They see it in corridors, in bathrooms, on the bus": UK schools 'porn crisis*. [online] The Guardian. Available at: https://www.theguardian.com/global-development/2021/dec/05/they-see-it-in-corridors-in-bathrooms-on-the-bus-uk-schools-porn-crisis. (Accessed 16 February, 2022).

[153] www.quodb.com. (n.d.). *QuoDB | The movie quotes database*. [online] QuoDB. Available at: https://www.quodb.com/search/porn. (Accessed 16 February, 2022).

[154] Television Academy. (n.d.). *Outstanding Childrens Program Nominees / Winners 2005*. [online] Emmys. Available at: https://www.emmys.com/awards/nominees-winners/2005/outstanding-childrens-program. (Accessed 16 February, 2022).

[155] Ofcom. (2021). *Online Nation 2021 Report*. [online] Ofcom. Available at: https://www.ofcom.org.uk/__data/assets/pdf_file/0013/220414/online-nation-2021-report.pdf. (Accessed 15 February, 2022).

[156] Pornhub. (n.d.). *2021 Year in Review – Pornhub Insights*. [online] Pornhub. Available at: https://www.pornhub.com/insights/yir-2021. (Accessed 1 February, 2022).

[157] Ofcom. (2021). *Online Nation 2021 Report*. [online] Ofcom. Available at: https://www.ofcom.org.uk/__data/assets/pdf_file/0013/220414/online-nation-2021-report.pdf. (Accessed 15 February, 2022).

[158] Moya Lothian-McLean (2019). *How do your porn habits compare with young people across Britain?* [online] BBC Three. Available at: https://www.bbc.co.uk/bbcthree/article/bb79a2ce-0de4-4965-98f0-9ebbcfcc2a60. (Accessed 16 February, 2022).

[159] Ofcom. (2021). *Online Nation 2021 Report.* [online] Ofcom. Available at: https://www.ofcom.org.uk/__data/assets/pdf_file/0013/220414/online-nation-2021-report.pdf. (Accessed 15 February, 2022).

[160] Martellozzo, E., Monaghan, A., Adler, J.R., Davidson, J., Leyva, R. and Horvath, M.A.H. (2016) *I wasn't sure it was normal to. watch it.* [online] NSPCC. Available at: https://learning.nspcc.org.uk/research-resources/2016/i-wasn-t-sure-it-was-normal-to-watch-it. (Accessed 16 February, 2022).

[161] BBFC (2019). *Children see pornography as young as seven, new report finds.* [online] BBFC. Available at: https://www.bbfc.co.uk/about-us/news/children-see-pornography-as-young-as-seven-new-report-finds. (Accessed 16 February, 2022).

[162] Loxton, Rachel. (2015). *Nearly one in 10 children aged 12-13 fear they are addicted to porn.* [online] Glasgow Times. Available at: https://www.glasgowtimes.co.uk/news/13305186.nearly-one-in-10-children-aged-12-13-fear-they-are-addicted-to-porn. (Accessed 16 February, 2022).

[163] Ibid.

[164] BBC News. (2017). *Girls go along with sex acts, says teacher.* [online] BBC News. Available at: https://www.bbc.co.uk/news/education-41499243. (Accessed 16 February, 2022).

[165] Ibid.

[166] Ibid.

[167] Pornhub. (n.d.). *2021 Year in Review – Pornhub Insights.* [online] Pornhub. Available at: https://www.pornhub.com/insights/yir-2021. (Accessed 1 February, 2022).

[168] Pornhub. (n.d.). *The 2019 Year in Review – Pornhub Insights.* [online] Pornhub. Available at: https://www.pornhub.com/insights/2019-year-in-review#searches. (Accessed 1 February, 2022).

[169] Tighe, Siobhann. (2017). *Is it OK to watch porn in public?* [online] BBC News. Available at: https://www.bbc.co.uk/news/magazine-38611265. (Accessed 16 February, 2022).

[170] Fight The New Drug. (2021). *"Real People are Gross": 3 Reasons Why Animated Porn is So Popular.* [online] Fight The New Drug. Available at: https://fightthenewdrug.org/animated-porn-is-gaining-popularity. (Accessed 16 February, 2022).

[171] *Who Framed Roger Rabbit?* (1988). [Motion Picture] Touchstone Pictures.

[172] Ofcom. (2021). *Online Nation 2021 Report.* [online] Ofcom. Available at: https://www.ofcom.org.uk/__data/assets/pdf_file/0013/220414/online-nation-2021-report.pdf. (Accessed 15 February, 2022).

[173] Perry, S.L. and Schleifer, C. (2017). *Till Porn Do Us Part? A Longitudinal Examination of Pornography Use and Divorce.* The Journal of Sex Research, 55(3), pp.284–296. [online] Enough. Available at: https://www.enough.org/objects/Till_Porn_Do_Us_Part_A_Longitudinal_Exam_fnv.pdf. (Accessed 15 February, 2022).

[174] Willoughby BJ, Carroll JS, Busby DM, Brown CC. Differences in Pornography Use Among Couples: Associations with Satisfaction, Stability, and Relationship Processes. Arch Sex Behav. 2016 Jan;45(1):145-58. doi: 10.1007/s10508-015-0562-9. Epub 2015 Jul 31. PMID: 26228990.

[175] Marateck, J. (2018). *Online dating lowers self-esteem, increases depression.* [online] CNN. Available at: https://edition.cnn.com/2018/05/29/health/online-dating-depression-study/index.html. (Accessed 16 February, 2022).

[176] Business Wire. (2020). *New Report from Facemoji Keyboard Shows Most Popular Emoji on Dating Apps in the US.* [online] Business Wire. Available at: https://www.businesswire.com/news/home/2020021100

5126/en/New-Report-from-Facemoji-Keyboard-Shows-Most-Popular-Emoji-on-Dating-Apps-in-the-US. (Accessed 16 February, 2022).

[177] Vogels, E.A. (2020). *10 facts about Americans and online dating*. [online] Pew Research Center. Available at: https://www.pewresearch.org/fact-tank/2020/02/06/10-facts-about-americans-and-online-dating. (Accessed 16 February, 2022).

[178] Ibid.

[179] Ibid.

[180] APA. (2016). *Tinder: Swiping Self Esteem?* [online] APA. Available at: https://www.apa.org/news/press/releases/2016/08/tinder-self-esteem. (Accessed 16 February, 2022).

[181] Ibid.

[182] Tinder Newsroom. (2021). *Tinder Launches Newest Experience In Explore - Music Mode*. [online] Tinder Press Room. Available at: https://www.tinderpressroom.com/Tinder-Launches-Newest-Experience-In-Explore-Music-Mode. (Accessed 16 February, 2022).

[183] Tinder. (2022). *Find out why Tinder® is the world's best dating app*. [online] Tinder. Available at: https://tinder.com/en-GB/about-tinder. (Accessed 16 February, 2022).

[184] Meshi, D., Elizarova, A., Bender, A. and Verdejo-Garcia, A. (2019). Excessive social media users demonstrate impaired decision making in the Iowa Gambling Task. *Journal of Behavioral Addictions*, 8(1), pp.169–173. [online] Social & Media Neuroscience Lab. Available at: http://smnlab.msu.edu/wp-content/uploads/2019/01/Meshi_2019_JBehavAddict.pdf. (Accessed 16 February, 2022).

[185] Haynes, T. (2018). *Dopamine, Smartphones & You: A battle for your time*. [online] Science in the News. Available at: https://sitn.hms.harvard.edu/flash/2018/dopamine-smartphones-battle-time. (Accessed 16 February, 2022).

[186] Marcotte AS, Kaufman EM, Campbell JT, Reynolds TA, Garcia JR, Gesselman AN. Sextech Use as a Potential Mental Health Reprieve: The Role of Anxiety, Depression, and Loneliness in Seeking Sex Online. *International Journal of Environmental Research and Public Health*. 2021; 18(17):8924. https://doi.org/10.3390/ijerph18178924.

[187] Bőthe, B., Tóth-Király, I., Bella, N., Potenza, M. N., Demetrovics, Z., & Orosz, G. (2021). Why do people watch pornography? The motivational basis of pornography use. *Psychology of Addictive Behaviors, 35*(2), 172–186. https://doi.org/10.1037/adb0000603.

[188] Sniewski, L., & Farvid, P. (2020). Hidden in shame: Heterosexual men's experiences of self-perceived problematic pornography use. *Psychology of Men & Masculinities, 21*(2), 201–212. https://doi.org/10.1037/men0000232.

[189] Kühn, S., & Gallinat, J. (2014). Brain structure and functional connectivity associated with pornography consumption: the brain on porn. *JAMA psychiatry, 71*(7), 827–834. https://doi.org/10.1001/jamapsychiatry.2014.93.

[190] Wolf, Naomi. (2003). *Naomi Wolf on Why Porn Turns Men Off the Real Thing*. [online] New York Magazine. Available at: https://nymag.com/nymetro/news/trends/n_9437. (Accessed 16 February, 2022).

[191] Waterson, Jim. (2019). *UK's porn age-verification rules can be circumvented in minutes*. [online] The Guardian. Available at: https://www.theguardian.com/society/2019/apr/19/uks-porn-age-verification-rules-can-be-circumvented-in-minutes. (Accessed 16 February, 2022).

[192] AP News. (2021). *German court OKs ban on Cyprus-based porn sites*. [online] AP News. Available at: https://apnews.com/article/entertainment-business-europe-germany-european-union-

8b9d9a7d5c1f59dc7440a64690f40268. (Accessed 16 February, 2022).

[193] NCOSE. (2021). *France to Block Pornography Tube Sites for Lax Age Verification Controls*. [online] End Sexual Exploitation. Available at: https://endsexualexploitation.org/articles/france-to-block-pornography-tube-sites-for-lax-age-verification-controls. (Accessed 16 February, 2022).

[194] Waterson, Jim. (2022). *Reddit and Twitter users face age checks under UK porn law plans*. [online] The Guardian. Available at: https://www.theguardian.com/society/2022/feb/09/reddit-and-twitter-users-face-age-checks-under-uk-porn-law-plans. (Accessed 16 February, 2022).

[195] Milmo, Dan and Waterson, Jim. (2022). *Porn sites in UK will have to check ages in planned update to online safety bill*. [online] The Guardian. Available at: https://www.theguardian.com/society/2022/feb/08/porn-sites-in-uk-will-have-to-check-ages-in-planned-update-to-online-safety-bill. (Accessed 16 February, 2022).

[196] Waterson, Jim. (2022). *Reddit and Twitter users face age checks under UK porn law plans*. [online] The Guardian. Available at: https://www.theguardian.com/society/2022/feb/09/reddit-and-twitter-users-face-age-checks-under-uk-porn-law-plans. (Accessed 16 February, 2022).

[197] Hawkins, Dawn. (2020). *Millions of abuse videos removed in hours! NCOSE named as major reason*. [online] End Sexual Exploitation. Available at: https://endsexualexploitation.org/articles/millions-of-abuse-videos-removed-in-hours-ncose-named-as-major-reason. (Accessed 16 February, 2022).

[198] @Pornhub. (2020). *https://twitter.com/pornhub/status/1266929094329016325*. [online] Twitter. Available at: https://twitter.com/Pornhub/status/126692909432901632 5. (Accessed 16 February, 2022).

[199] Fight The New Drug. (2021). *Content on Pornhub Reportedly Normalizes and Promotes Racism and Racist Stereotypes*. [online] Fight the New Drug. Available at: https://fightthenewdrug.org/porn-content-normalizes-promotes-racism-racist-stereotypes. (Accessed 16 February, 2022).

[200] @Pornhub. (2020). *https://twitter.com/pornhub/status/1266929204848984064*. [online] Twitter. Available at: https://twitter.com/Pornhub/status/1266929204848984064. (Accessed 16 February, 2022).

[201] Fight The New Drug. (2021). *Content on Pornhub Reportedly Normalizes and Promotes Racism and Racist Stereotypes*. [online] Fight the New Drug. Available at: https://fightthenewdrug.org/porn-content-normalizes-promotes-racism-racist-stereotypes. (Accessed 16 February, 2022).

[202] www.pornhub.com. (2021). *The latest on our commitment to trust and safety*. [online] Pornhub. Available at: https://www.pornhub.com/blog/11422. (Accessed 16 February, 2022).

[203] Hedges, Chris. (2009). *Empire of Illusion: The End of Literacy and the Triumph of Spectacle*. [Book] Bold Type Books.

[204] Elan, Riya. (2022). *Dystopia-core: what is the new pandemic-era punk look?* [online] The Guardian. Available at: https://www.theguardian.com/fashion/2022/jan/17/dystopia-core-what-is-new-pandemic-era-punk-look-fashion. (Accessed 16 February, 2022).

[205] Ibid.

[206] Instagram. (2021). *Instagram Trends for 2022 - See What's Trending for Gen-Z in 2022 | Instagram Blog*. [online] Instagram. Available at: https://about.instagram.com/blog/announcements/instagram-trends-2022. (Accessed 16 February, 2022).

[207] Lavin, Will. (2020). *Cardi B responds to Carol Baskin's "WAP" criticism: "That's just ridiculous."* [online] NME.

Available at:
https://www.nme.com/en_asia/news/music/cardi-b-responds-to-carol-baskins-wap-criticism-2729746.
(Accessed 16 February, 2022).

[208] *WAP*. (2020). Cardi B feat. Megan Thee Stallion. [Music] Atlantic Records.

[209] @iamcardib. (2021). *https://twitter.com/iamcardib/status/134624956676550 2465*. [online] Twitter. Available at: https://twitter.com/iamcardib/status/1346249566765502 465. (Accessed 16 February, 2022).

[210] Ofcom. (2021). *Online Nation 2021 Report*. [online] Ofcom. Available at: https://www.ofcom.org.uk/__data/assets/pdf_file/0013/220414/online-nation-2021-report.pdf. (Accessed 15 February, 2022).

[211] Nostro, Lauren. (2014). *Nicki Minaj Talks Fear Of Losing Privacy And Keeping Drake In The Friendzone Forever*. [online] Complex. Available at: https://www.complex.com/covers/nicki-minaj-interview-2014-cover-story. (Accessed 8 April, 2022).

[212] Karsay, K., Matthes, J., Buchsteiner, L., & Grosser, V. (2019). Increasingly sexy? Sexuality and sexual objectification in popular music videos, 1995–2016. *Psychology of Popular Media Culture, 8*(4), 346–357. https://doi.org/10.1037/ppm0000221.

[213] Kathrin Karsay, Jörg Matthes, Phillip Platzer & Myrna Plinke (2018) *Adopting the Objectifying Gaze: Exposure to Sexually Objectifying Music Videos and Subsequent Gazing Behavior,* Media Psychology, 21:1, 27-49, DOI: 10.1080/15213269.2017.1378110.

[214] Jennifer Stevens Aubrey, K. Megan Hopper & Wanjiru G. Mbure (2011) *Check That Body! The Effects of Sexually Objectifying Music Videos on College Men's Sexual Beliefs,* Journal of Broadcasting & Electronic Media, 55:3, 360-379, DOI: 10.1080/08838151.2011.597469.

[215] Ainsley, Helen. (2020). *Cardi B & Megan Thee Stallion's WAP claims third week at Number 1*. [online]

Official Charts. Available at:
https://www.officialcharts.com/chart-news/cardi-b-and-megan-thee-stallions-wap-makes-it-three-weeks-at-uk-number-1__31010. (Accessed 16 February, 2022).

216 Mitchell, Molli. (2022). *Here's who won "Too Hot To Handle" Season 3 and how much money was left.* [online] Newsweek. Available at:
https://www.newsweek.com/who-won-too-hot-handle-season-3-how-much-money-was-left-harry-beaux-1670807. (Accessed 16 February, 2022).

217 Netflix (2020). *Too Hot To Handle | Season 1 | Official Trailer | Netflix. YouTube.* Available at:
https://www.youtube.com/watch?v=2JgPJpgnut4. (Accessed 1 February, 2022).

218 Too Hot To Handle. Season 1. (2020). *Two's a Company, Three's a… Threesome.* [TV Show] Netflix.

219 Too Hot To Handle. Season 1. (2020). *Lust or Bust.* [TV Show] Netflix.

220 Too Hot To Handle. Season 2. (2021). *C**kblocked by a Cone.* [TV Show] Netflix.

221 D'Addario, Daniel. (2017). *"Game of Thrones": Inside the World's Most Popular Show.* [online] TIME. Available at: https://time.com/game-of-thrones-2017. (Accessed 16 February, 2022).

222 *Pam & Tommy.* (2022). [TV Show] Hulu.

223 Martin, L. (2022). *Pam & Tommy review: The sex-tape drama feels exploitative.* [online] BBC. Available at:
https://www.bbc.com/culture/article/20220126-pam-tommy-review-the-sex-tape-drama-feels-exploitative. (Accessed 16 February, 2022).

224 BBC News. (2022). *Neil Parish MP: I'm resigning after porn moment of madness.* [Online] BBC News. Available at: https://www.bbc.co.uk/news/uk-politics-61284686. (Accessed April 30th, 2022).

225 *Thank You For Smoking.* (2005). [Motion Picture] Fox Searchlight Pictures.

226 Goodhart, Benjie. (2022). *"At 6pm every evening the screen went blank": the outlandish tale of the UK's TV*

blackout. [online] The Guardian. Available at:
https://www.theguardian.com/tv-and-radio/2022/feb/16/at-6pm-every-evening-the-screen-went-blank-the-outlandish-tale-of-the-uks-tv-blackout.
(Accessed 16 February, 2022).

227 UK Parliament. (n.d.). *Television and Radio Broadcasting. (Hansard, 19 January 1972).* [online] UK Parliament. Available at:
https://api.parliament.uk/historic-hansard/commons/1972/jan/19/television-and-radio-broadcasting-1. (Accessed 16 February, 2022).

228 Ofcom. (2021). *Full stream ahead: Brits spend a third of 2020 watching TV and video.* [online] Ofcom. Available at: https://www.ofcom.org.uk/about-ofcom/latest/media/media-releases/2021/brits-spend-a-third-of-2020-watching-tv-and-video. (Accessed 16 February, 2022).

229 *Thank You For Smoking.* (2005). [Motion Picture] Fox Searchlight Pictures.

230 Netflix. *How to use "Play Something."* [online] Netflix. Available at: https://help.netflix.com/en/node/119162. (Accessed 16 February, 2022).

231 Ofcom. (2021). *Full stream ahead: Brits spend a third of 2020 watching TV and video.* [online] Ofcom. Available at: https://www.ofcom.org.uk/about-ofcom/latest/media/media-releases/2021/brits-spend-a-third-of-2020-watching-tv-and-video. (Accessed 16 February, 2022).

232 BARB. (2020). *TV since 1981. Year 2018. | BARB.* [online] BARB. Available at:
https://www.barb.co.uk/resources/tv-facts/tv-since-1981/2018/top10. (Accessed February 16, 2022).

233 BARB. (2020). *TV since 1981. Year 2019. | BARB.* [online] BARB. Available at:
https://www.barb.co.uk/resources/tv-facts/tv-since-1981/2019/top10. (Accessed February 16, 2022).

234 Buckman, Adam. (2017). *And That's That: "The O'Reilly Factor" Is No More.* [online] Media Post.

Available at:
https://www.mediapost.com/publications/article/299478/and-thats-that-the-oreilly-factor-is-no-more.html. (Accessed February 16, 2022).

235 Premier League. (n.d.). *A record-breaking season.* [online] Premier League. Available at: https://www.premierleague.com/season-review/the-fans/2164581?articleId=2164581. (Accessed 15 February, 2022).

236 BBC News. (2021). *BBC star salaries: Gary Lineker still BBC's top earner despite pay cut.* [online] BBC News. Available at: https://www.bbc.co.uk/news/entertainment-arts-57722068. (Accessed 16 February, 2022).

237 @GaryLineker. (2022). *https://twitter.com/garylineker/status/14827192169983 71329.* [online] Twitter. Available at: https://twitter.com/GaryLineker/status/14827192169983 71329. (Accessed 16 February, 2022).

238 Cummins, Joseph. (2022). *What is the future of the BBC's funding model? | Media news.* [online] Journalism.co.uk. Available at: https://www.journalism.co.uk/news/what-is-the-future-of-the-bbc-s-funding-model-/s2/a895526. (Accessed 16 February, 2022).

239 West Ham United Fan Token (WESTHAM). (n.d.). *West Ham United Fan Token.* [online] Available at: https://westhamfc.net. (Accessed 26 March, 2022).

240 VeVe Digital Collectibles. (2022). *Marvel Digital Comics — Deadpool #1.* [online] Medium. Available at: https://medium.com/veve-collectibles/marvel-digital-comics-deadpool-1-5a6d7b7af381. (Accessed 27 March, 2022).

241 Marvel Entertainment. (n.d.). *Deadpool (1997) #-1 | Comic Issues | Marvel.* [online] Marvel. Available at: https://www.marvel.com/comics/issue/8461/deadpool_1 997_-1. (Accessed 27 March, 2022).

242 OliCrypto. (n.d.). *Professional Female Tennis Player - Right Arm & Shoulder - Lifetime Tattoo & Body Art*

Rights. [online] OpenSea. Available at:
https://opensea.io/assets/0x495f947276749ce646f68ac8c
248420045cb7b5e/739151596722054398061656596762941167674328040257150862068093791482477816053377.
(Accessed 27 March, 2022).

²⁴³ Caron, Emily. (2021). *Croatian Tennis Player Sells Ad Space for an Arm and a NFT*. [online] Yahoo Sports. Available at: https://sports.yahoo.com/croatian-tennis-pro-sells-ad-140015116.html. (Accessed 27 March, 2022).

²⁴⁴ The Boys. Season 2. (2020). *The Big Ride*. [TV Show] Amazon Prime Video.

²⁴⁵ Marti Renti. (n.d.). *Home | Marti Renti*. [online] Marti Renti. Available at: https://martirenti.com. (Accessed 27 March, 2022).

²⁴⁶ Syed, Armani. (2021). *An influencer sold her love as an NFT for $250,000 and is going to have dinner with the mystery buyer*. [online] Insider. Available at: https://www.insider.com/influencer-sold-love-as-nft-dinner-with-mystery-buyer-2021-7. (Accessed 27 March, 2022).

²⁴⁷ *Ibid*.

²⁴⁸ Marti Renti. (n.d.). *Home | Marti Renti*. [online] Marti Renti. Available at: https://martirenti.com. (Accessed 27 March, 2022).

²⁴⁹ Syed, Armani. (2021). *An influencer sold her love as an NFT for $250,000 and is going to have dinner with the mystery buyer*. [online] Insider. Available at: https://www.insider.com/influencer-sold-love-as-nft-dinner-with-mystery-buyer-2021-7. (Accessed 27 March, 2022).

²⁵⁰ Fanadise. (2021). *First ever NFT Love!* [online] YouTube. Available at: https://www.youtube.com/watch?v=FUaZ27zRVg0&t=25s. (Accessed 27 March, 2022).

²⁵¹ Ibid.

²⁵² Benstead, S. and Almeida, L. (2022). *Is Bitcoin a good investment in 2022?* [online] The Telegraph. Available at: https://www.telegraph.co.uk/investing/shares/bitcoin-

price-usd-gbp-prediction-news-crypto-what-buy-2022. (Accessed 27 March, 2022).

253 Renteria, N., Wilson, T. and Strohecker, K. (2021). *In a world first, El Salvador makes bitcoin legal tender.* [online] Reuters. Available at: https://www.reuters.com/world/americas/el-salvador-approves-first-law-bitcoin-legal-tender-2021-06-09. (Accessed 27 March, 2022).

254 Crane, Emily. (2021). *El Salvador's president declares himself world's "coolest dictator."* [online] New York Post. Available at: https://nypost.com/2021/09/22/el-salvadors-president-declares-himself-worlds-coolest-dictator. (Accessed 27 March, 2022).

255 Silver, Katie. (2021). *Bitcoin crashes on first day as El Salvador's legal tender.* [online] BBC News. Available at: https://www.bbc.co.uk/news/business-58459098. (Accessed 27 March, 2022).

256 Balcáceres, Pablo. (2022). *Why Bitcoin Is Losing Its Shine in El Salvador.* [online] Bloomberg Línea. Available at: https://www.bloomberglinea.com/2022/03/14/why-bitcoin-is-losing-its-shine-in-el-salvador. (Accessed 27 March, 2022).

257 Hetzner, Christiaan. (2022). *El Salvador's millennial president launching bitcoin "volcano bond" in major bet on cryptocurrency craze.* [online] Fortune. Available at: https://fortune.com/2022/03/14/el-salvador-president-bitcoin-city-volcano-bond-nayib-bukele. (Accessed 27 March, 2022).

258 Pozzebon, Stefano. (2021). *Analysis: The political drama raising fears about El Salvador's democracy.* [online] CNN. Available at: https://edition.cnn.com/2021/05/05/americas/el-salvadors-political-crisis-intl-latam/index.html. (Accessed 27 March, 2022).

259 Specht, Doug. (2019). *El Salvador: young maverick Bukele wins presidential election, but country's future remains uncertain.* [online] The Conversation. Available

at: https://theconversation.com/el-salvador-young-maverick-bukele-wins-presidential-election-but-countrys-future-remains-uncertain-111775. (Accessed 27 March, 2022).

260 Milmo, Dan. (2022). *Ukraine to launch NFT to mark history of Russian invasion.* [online] The Guardian. Available at: https://www.theguardian.com/world/2022/mar/13/ukraine-nft-history-of-russian-invasion-war. (Accessed 27 March, 2022).

261 Ministry of Digital Transformation of Ukraine. (2022). *Aid For Ukraine – Donate Crypto to Ukraine.* [online] Donate Ministry of Digital Transformation of Ukraine. Available at: https://donate.thedigital.gov.ua. (Accessed 27 March, 2022).

262 Tidy, Joe. (2022). *Twitter is part of our war effort - Ukraine minister.* [online] BBC News. Available at: https://www.bbc.co.uk/news/technology-60608222 [Accessed 27 March, 2022].

263 Datskevych, Natalia. (2022). *Over 50 IT companies join Ukraine's "special tax regime" Diia City in first three days.* [online] The Kyiv Independent. Available at: https://kyivindependent.com/tech/over-50-it-companies-join-ukraines-special-economic-zone-diia-city-in-its-first-days. (Accessed 27 March, 2022).

264 Race, Michael & Thomas, Daniel. (2022). *Cryptocurrency: UK Treasury to regulate some stablecoins.* [online] BBC News. Available at: https://www.bbc.co.uk/news/business-60983561. (Accessed 15 April, 2022).

265 Ibid.

266 Kharpal, Arjun. (2022). *China's tech giants push toward an $8 trillion metaverse opportunity — one that will be highly regulated.* [online] CNBC. Available at: https://www.cnbc.com/2022/02/14/china-metaverse-tech-giants-latest-moves-regulatory-action.html. (Accessed 27 March, 2022).

267 Ibid.

[268] *Ready Player One.* (2018). [Motion Picture] Warner Bros. Pictures.

[269] *Californication.* (1999). Red Hot Chili Peppers. [Music] Warner Bros. Records.

[270] *Fight Club.* (1999). [Motion Picture] 20th Century Fox.

[271] BBC News. (2022). *Privatising Channel 4: What could new ownership mean and who might buy it?* [online] BBC News. Available at: https://www.bbc.co.uk/news/entertainment-arts-60993887. (Accessed 6 April, 2022).

[272] NHS (2021). *Rate of mental disorders among children remained stable in 2021 after previous rise, report shows.* [online] NHS Digital. Available at: https://digital.nhs.uk/news/2021/rate-of-mental-disorders-among-children-remained-stable-in-2021-after-previous-rise-report-shows. (Accessed 6 April, 2022).

Milton Keynes UK
Ingram Content Group UK Ltd.
UKHW041500021023
R3424000001B/R34240PG429652UKX00001B/1